THE MORAL OBLIGATION
TO BE INTELLIGENT

THE
MORAL OBLIGATION
TO BE INTELLIGENT
and Other Essays

BY

JOHN ERSKINE

Essay Index Reprint Series

BOOKS FOR LIBRARIES PRESS
FREEPORT, NEW YORK

First Published 1921
Reprinted 1969

STANDARD BOOK NUMBER:
8369-1291-8

LIBRARY OF CQNGRESS CATALOG CARD NUMBER:
70-93337

PRINTED IN THE UNITED STATES OF AMERICA

CONTENTS

NOTE

THE title essay, originally read before the Phi Beta Kappa Society of Amherst College, is reprinted with the editor's courteous permission from the *Hibbert Journal.* The last essay also was read before the Phi Beta Kappa Society of Amherst College, and before the Phi Beta Kappa Alumni of New York City.

In different ways the four essays set forth one theme—the moral use to which intelligence might be put, in rendering our admirations and our loyalties at once more sensible and more noble.

THE MORAL OBLIGATION
TO BE INTELLIGENT

THE MORAL OBLIGATION
TO BE INTELLIGENT

I

IF a wise man should ask, What are
the modern virtues? and should answer his own question by a summary of
the things we admire; if he should discard
as irrelevant the ideals which by tradition we profess, but which are not found
outside of the tradition or the profession
—ideals like meekness, humility, the re-
nunciation of this world; if he should
include only those excellences to which
our hearts are daily given, and by which
our conduct is motived,—in such an in-
ventory what virtues would he name?

THE MORAL OBLIGATION

This question is neither original nor very new. Our times await the reckoning up of our spiritual goods which is here suggested. We have at least this wisdom, that many of us are curious to know just what our virtues are. I wish I could offer myself as the wise man who brings the answer. But I raise this question merely to ask another—When the wise man brings his list of our genuine admirations, will intelligence be one of them? We might seem to be well within the old ideal of modesty if we claimed the virtue of intelligence. But before we claim the virtue, are we convinced that it is a virtue, not a peril?

II

The disposition to consider intelligence a peril is an old Anglo-Saxon inheritance. Our ancestors have celebrated this disposition in verse and prose. Splendid as our literature is, it has not voiced all the aspirations of humanity, nor could it be expected to voice an aspiration that has not characteristically belonged to the English race; the praise of intelligence is not one of its characteristic glories.

"Be good, sweet maid, and let who will be clever."

Here is the startling alternative which to the English, alone among great nations, has been not startling but a matter of course. Here is the casual assumption that a choice must be made between goodness and intelligence; that stupidity is first cousin to moral conduct, and cleverness the first step into mischief; that reason and God are not on good terms with each other; that the mind and the heart are rival buckets in the well of truth, inexorably balanced—full

[5]

mind, starved heart—stout heart, weak head.

Kingsley's line is a convenient text, but to establish the point that English literature voices a traditional distrust of the mind we must go to the masters. In Shakspere's plays there are some highly intelligent men, but they are either villains or tragic victims. To be as intelligent as Richard or Iago or Edmund seems to involve some break with goodness; to be as wise as Prospero seems to imply some Faust-like traffic with the forbidden world; to be as thoughtful as Hamlet seems to be too thoughtful to live. In Shakspere the prizes of life go to such men as Bassanio, or Duke Orsino, or Florizel—men of good conduct and sound character, but of no particular intelligence. There might, indeed, appear to be one general exception to this sweeping statement: Shakspere does concede intelligence as a fortunate possession to some of his heroines. But upon even a slight examination those ladies, like Portia, turn out to have been among Shakspere's Italian importations —their wit was part and parcel of the story he borrowed; or, like Viola, they are English types of humility, patience, and loyalty, such as we find in the old ballads, with a bit of Euphuism added, a foreign cleverness of speech. After all, these are only a few of Shakspere's heroines; over against them are Ophelia, Juliet, Desdemona, Hero, Cordelia, Miranda, Perdita—lovable for other qualities than intellect,—and in a sinister group, Lady Macbeth, Cleopatra, Goneril, intelligent and wicked.

In *Paradise Lost* Milton attributes intelligence of the highest order to the devil. That this is an Anglo-Saxon reading of the infernal character may be shown by a reference to the book of Job, where Satan is simply a troublesome body, and the great wisdom of the story is from the voice of God in the whirlwind. But Milton makes his Satan so thoughtful, so persistent and liberty-loving, so magnanimous, and God so illogical, so heartless and repressive, that many perfectly moral readers fear lest Milton, like the modern novelists, may have known good and evil, but could not tell them apart. It is disconcerting to intelligence that it should be God's angel who cautions Adam not to wander in the earth, nor inquire concerning heaven's causes and ends, and that it should be Satan meanwhile who questions and explores. By Milton's reckoning of intelligence the theologian and the scientist to-day alike take after Satan.

If there were time, we might trace this valuation of intelligence through the

English novel. We should see how often
the writers have distinguished between
intelligence and goodness, and have en-
listed our affections for a kind of inexpert
virtue. In Fielding or Scott, Thackeray
or Dickens, the hero of the English novel
is a well-meaning blunderer who in the
last chapter is temporarily rescued by the
grace of God from the mess he has made
of his life. Unless he also dies in the last
chapter, he will probably need rescue
again. The dear woman whom the hero
marries is, with a few notable exceptions,
rather less intelligent than himself. When
David Copperfield marries Agnes, his
prospects of happiness, to the eyes of
intelligence, look not very exhilarating.
Agnes has more sense than Dora, but it
is not even for that slight distinction
that we must admire her; her great
qualities are of the heart—patience, humility, faithfulness. These are the qual-

ities also of Thackeray's good heroines, like Laura or Lady Castlewood. Beatrice Esmond and Becky Sharp, both highly intelligent, are of course a bad lot.

No less significant is the kind of emotion the English novelist invites towards his secondary or lower-class heroes—toward Mr. Boffin in *Our Mutual Friend*, for example, or Harry Foker in *Pendennis*. These characters amuse us, and we feel pleasantly superior to them, but we agree with the novelist that they are wholly admirable in their station. Yet if a Frenchman—let us say Balzac—were presenting such types, he would make us feel, as in *Père Goriot* or *Eugénie Grandet*, not only admiration for the stable, loyal nature, but also deep pity that such goodness should be so tragically bound in unintelligence or vulgarity. This comparison of racial temperaments helps us to understand ourselves. We may continue the method

at our leisure. What would Socrates
have thought of Mr. Pickwick, or the
Vicar of Wakefield, or David Copperfield, or Arthur Pendennis? For that
matter, would he have felt admiration or
pity for Colonel Newcome?

III

I hardly need confess that this is not
an adequate account of English literature. Let me hasten to say that I know
the reader is resenting this somewhat
cavalier handling of the noble writers
he loves. He probably is wondering
how I can expect to increase his love
of literature by such unsympathetic remarks. But just now I am not con-
cerned about our love of literature; I
take it for granted, and use it as an instrument to prod us with. If we love
Shakspere and Milton and Scott and

Dickens and Thackeray, and yet do not know what qualities their books hold out for our admiration, then—let me say it as delicately as possible—our admiration is not discriminating; and if we neither have discrimination nor are disturbed by our lack of it, then perhaps that wise man could not list intelligence among our virtues. Certainly it would be but a silly account of English literature to say only that it set little store by the things of the mind. I am aware that for the sake of my argument I have exaggerated, by insisting upon only one aspect of English literature. But our history betrays a peculiar warfare between character and intellect, such as to the Greek, for example, would have been incomprehensible. The great Englishman, like the most famous Greeks, had intelligence as well as character, and was at ease with them both. But whereas

the notable Greek seems typical of his
race, the notable Englishman usually
seems an exception to his own people, and
is often best appreciated in other lands.
What is more singular—in spite of the
happy combination in himself of character and intelligence, he often fails to
recognize the value of that combination
in his neighbors. When Shakspere portrayed such amateurish statesmen as the
Duke in *Measure for Measure*, Burleigh
was guiding Elizabeth's empire, and Francis Bacon was soon to be King James's
counsellor. It was the young Milton
who pictured the life of reason in *L'Allegro*
and *Il Penseroso*, the most spiritual fruit
of philosophy in *Comus;* and when he
wrote his epic he was probably England's
most notable example of that intellectual
inquiry and independence which in his
great poem he discouraged. There remain several well-known figures in our

literary history who have both possessed and believed in intelligence—
Byron and Shelley in what seems our own
day, Edmund Spenser before Shakspere's
time. England has more or less neglected
all three, but they must in fairness be
counted to her credit. Some excuse
might be offered for the neglect of Byron
and Shelley by a nation that likes the
proprieties; but the gentle Spenser, the
noblest philosopher and most chivalrous
gentleman in our literature, seems to be
unread only because he demands a mind
as well as a heart used to high things.

This will be sufficient qualification of
any disparagement of English literature;
no people and no literature can be great
that are not intelligent, and England
has produced not only statesmen and
scientists of the first order, but also poets
in whom the soul was fitly mated with a
lofty intellect. But I am asking you to

reconsider your reading in history and fiction, to reflect whether our race has usually thought highly of the intelligence by which it has been great; I suggest these non-intellectual aspects of our literature as commentary upon my question—and all this with the hope of pressing upon you the question as to what *you* think of intelligence.

Those of us who frankly prefer character to intelligence are therefore not without precedent. If we look beneath the history of the English people, beneath the ideas expressed in our literature, we find in the temper of our remotest ancestors a certain bias which still prescribes our ethics and still prejudices us against the mind. The beginnings of our conscience can be geographically located. It began in the German forests, and it gave its allegiance not to the intellect but to the will. Whether or not the severity of life in a hard climate raised the value of that persistence by which alone life could be preserved, the Germans as Tacitus knew them, and the Saxons as they landed in England, held as their chief virtue that will-power which makes character. For craft or strategy they had no use; they were already a bulldog race; they liked fighting, and they liked best to settle the matter hand to hand. The admiration for brute force which naturally accompanied this ideal of self-reliance, drew with it as naturally a certain moral sanction. A man was as good as his word, and he was ready to back up his word with a blow. No German, Tacitus says, would enter into a treaty of public or private business without his sword in his hand. When this emphasis upon the will became a social emphasis, it gave the direction to ethical feeling. Honor lay

in a man's integrity, in his willingness
and ability to keep his word; therefore
the man became more important than his
word or deed. Words and deeds were
then easily interpreted, not in terms of
absolute good and evil, but in terms of
the man behind them. The deeds of a
bad man were bad; the deeds of a good
man were good. Fielding wrote *Tom
Jones* to show that a good man sometimes does a bad action, consciously or
unconsciously, and a bad man sometimes does good, intentionally or unin-
tentionally. From the fact that *Tom
Jones* is still popularly supposed to be as
wicked as it is coarse, we may judge that
Fielding did not convert all his readers.
Some progress certainly has been made;
we do not insist that the more saintly of
two surgeons shall operate on us for ap-
pendicitis. But as a race we seem as
far as possible from realising that an

action can intelligently be called good
only if it contributes to a good end;
that it is the moral obligation of an intelligent creature to find out as far as
possible whether a given action leads to
a good or a bad end; and that any system of ethics that excuses him from that
obligation is vicious. If I give you
poison, meaning to give you wholesome
food, I have—to say the least—not done
a good act; and unless I intend to throw
overboard all pretence to intelligence, I
must feel some responsibility for that
trifling neglect to find out whether what
I gave you was food or poison.

Obvious as the matter is in this
academic illustration, it ought to have
been still more obvious in Matthew
Arnold's famous plea for culture. The
purpose of culture, he said, is "to make
reason and the will of God prevail."
This formula he quoted from an English-

man. Differently stated, the purpose of
culture, he said, is "to make an intelligent being yet more intelligent." This
formula he borrowed from a Frenchman.
The basis culture must have in character,
the English resolution to make reason
and the will of God prevail, Arnold took
for granted; no man ever set a higher
price on character—so far as character
by itself will go. But he spent his life
trying to sow a little suspicion that before
we can make the will of God prevail we
must find out what is the will of God.

I doubt if Arnold taught us much.
He merely embarrassed us temporarily.
Our race has often been so embarrassed
when it has turned a sudden corner and
come upon intelligence. Charles Kingsley himself, who would rather be good
than clever,—and had his wish,—was
temporarily embarrassed when in the
consciousness of his own upright char-

acter he publicly called Newman a liar.
Newman happened to be intelligent as
well as good, and Kingsley's discomfiture
is well known. But we discovered long
ago how to evade the sudden embarrass-
ments of intelligence. "Toll for the
brave," sings the poet for those who
went down in the *Royal George*. They
were brave. But he might have sung,
"Toll for the stupid." In order to clean
the hull, brave Kempenfelt and his eight
hundred heroes took the serious risk of
laying the vessel well over on its side,
while most of the crew were below.
Having made the error, they all died
bravely; and our memory passes easily
over the lack of a virtue we never did
think much of, and dwells on the English
virtues of courage and discipline. So
we forget the shocking blunder of the
charge of the Light Brigade, and proudly
sing the heroism of the victims. Lest

we flatter ourselves that this trick of defence has departed with our fathers— this reading of stupidity in terms of the tragic courage that endures its results— let us reflect that recently, after full warning, we drove a ship at top speed through a field of icebergs. When we were thrilled to read how superbly those hundreds died, in the great English way, a man pointed out that they did indeed die in the English way, and that our pride was therefore ill-timed; that all that bravery was wasted; that the tragedy was in the shipwreck of intelligence. That discouraging person was an Irishman.

IV

I have spoken of our social inheritance as though it were entirely English. Once more let me qualify my terms. Even

those ancestors of ours who never left
Great Britain were heirs of many civiliza-
tions—Roman, French, Italian, Greek.
With each world-tide some love of pure
intelligence was washed up on English
shores, and enriched the soil, and here
and there the old stock marvelled at its
own progeny. But to America, much
as we may sentimentally deplore it,
England seems destined to be less and
less the source of culture, of religion and
learning. Our land assimilates all races;
with every ship in the harbor our old
English ways of thought must crowd a
little closer to make room for a new tradition. If some of us do not greatly err,
these newcomers are chiefly driving to the
wall our inherited criticism of the intellect. As surely as the severe northern
climate taught our forefathers the value
of the will, the social conditions from
which these new citizens have escaped

have taught them the power of the mind.
They differ from each other, but against
the Anglo-Saxon they are confederated
in a Greek love of knowledge, in a Greek
assurance that sin and misery are the
fruit of ignorance, and that to know is to
achieve virtue. They join forces at once
with that earlier arrival from Greece,
the scientific spirit, which like all the
immigrants has done our hard work and
put up with our contempt. Between
this rising host that follow intelligence,
and the old camp that put their trust in a
stout heart, a firm will, and a strong hand,
the fight is on. Our college men will be
in the thick of it. If they do not take
sides, they will at least be battered in the
scuffle. At this moment they are readily
divided into those who wish to be men—
whatever that means—and those who
wish to be intelligent men, and those
who, unconscious of blasphemy or hu-

mor, prefer not to be intelligent, but to do the will of God.

When we consider the nature of the problems to be solved in our day, it seems—to many of us, at least—that these un-English arrivals are correct, that intelligence is the virtue we particularly need. Courage and steadfastness we cannot do without, so long as two men dwell on the earth; but it is time to discriminate in our praise of these virtues. If you want to get out of prison, what you need is the key to the lock. If you cannot get that, have courage and steadfastness. Perhaps the modern world has got into a kind of prison, and what is needed is the key to the lock. If none of the old virtues exactly fits, why should it seem ignoble to admit it? England for centuries has got on better by sheer character than some other nations by sheer intelligence, but there is after all a relation between the kind of problem and the means we should select to solve it. Not all problems are solved by will-power. When England overthrew Bonaparte, it was not his intelligence she overthrew; the contest involved other things besides intelligence, and she wore him out in the matter of physical endurance. The enemy that comes to her as a visible host or armada she can still close with and throttle; but when the foe arrives as an arrow that flieth by night, what avail the old sinews, the old stoutness of heart! We Americans face the same problems, and are too much inclined to oppose to them similar obsolete armor. We make a moral issue of an economic or social question, because it seems ignoble to admit it is simply a question for intelligence. Like the medicine-man, we use oratory and invoke our hereditary divinities, when the patient needs only a little quiet, or permission to get out of bed. We applaud those leaders who warm to their work—who, when they cannot open a door, threaten to kick it in. In the philosopher's words, we curse the obstacles of life as though they were devils. But they are not devils. They are obstacles.

V

Perhaps my question as to what you think of intelligence has been pushed far enough. But I cannot leave the subject without a confession of faith.

None of the reasons here suggested will quite explain the true worship of intelligence, whether we worship it as the scientific spirit, or as scholarship, or as any other reliance upon the mind. We really seek intelligence not for the answers it may suggest to the problems of

life, but because we believe it is life,—
not for aid in making the will of God
prevail, but because we believe it is the
will of God. We love it, as we love virtue, for its own sake, and we believe it is
only virtue's other and more precise
name. We believe that the virtues wait
upon intelligence—literally wait, in the
history of the race. Whatever is elemental in man—love, hunger, fear—has
obeyed from the beginning the discipline
of intelligence. We are told that to kill
one's aging parents was once a demonstra-
tion of solicitude; about the same time,
men hungered for raw meat and feared
the sun's eclipse. Filial love, hunger,
and fear are still motives to conduct,
but intelligence has directed them to
other ends. If we no longer hang the
thief or flog the school-boy, it is not
that we think less harshly of theft or
laziness, but that intelligence has found

a better persuasion to honesty and enterprise.

We believe that even in religion, in the most intimate room of the spirit, intelligence long ago proved itself the master-virtue. Its inward office from the beginning was to decrease fear and increase opportunity; its outward effect was to rob the altar of its sacrifice and the priest of his mysteries. Little wonder that from the beginning the disinterestedness of the accredited custodians of all temples has been tested by the kind of welcome they gave to intelligence. How many hecatombs were offered on more shores than that of Aulis, by seamen waiting for a favorable wind, before intelligence found out a boat that could tack! The altar was deserted, the religion revised—fear of the uncontrollable changing into delight in the knowledge that is power. We contemplate with satisfaction the law

by which in our long history one religion has driven out another, as one
hypothesis supplants another in astron-
omy or mathematics. The faith that
needs the fewest altars, the hypothesis
that leaves least unexplained, survives;
and the intelligence that changes most
fears into opportunity is most divine.

We believe this beneficent operation
of intelligence was swerving not one
degree from its ancient course when un-
der the name of the scientific spirit it
once more laid its influence upon religion. If the shock here seemed too
violent, if the purpose of intelligence here
seemed to be not revision but contradic-
tion, it was only because religion was
invited to digest an unusually large
amount of intelligence all at once. Moreover, it is not certain that devout people were more shocked by Darwinism
than the pious mariners were by the

first boat that could tack. Perhaps
the sacrifices were not abandoned all at
once.

But the lover of intelligence must be
patient with those who cannot readily
share his passion. Some pangs the mind
will inflict upon the heart. It is a mistake to think that men are united by
elemental affections. Our affections di-
vide us. We strike roots in immediate
time and space, and fall in love with our
locality, the customs and the language in
which we were brought up. Intelligence
unites us with mankind, by leading us in
sympathy to other times, other places,
other customs; but first the prejudiced
roots of affection must be pulled up.
These are the old pangs of intelligence,
which still comes to set a man at vari-
ance against his father, saying, "He that
loveth father or mother more than me, is
not worthy of me."

Yet, if intelligence begins in a pang, it proceeds to a vision. Through measureless time its office has been to make of life an opportunity, to make goodness articulate, to make virtue a fact. In history at least, if not yet in the individual, Plato's faith has come true, that sin is but ignorance, and knowledge and virtue are one. But all that intelligence has accomplished dwindles in comparison with the vision it suggests and warrants. Beholding this long liberation of the human spirit, we foresee, in every new light of the mind, one unifying mind, wherein the human race shall know its destiny and proceed to it with satisfaction, as an idea moves to its proper conclusion; we conceive of intelligence at last as the infinite order, wherein man, when he enters it, shall find himself.

Meanwhile he continues to find his

virtues by successive insights into his needs. Let us cultivate insight.

"O Wisdom of the Most High,
    That reachest from the beginning to the end,
    And dost order all things in strength and grace,
    Teach us now the way of understanding."

THE CALL TO SERVICE

THE CALL TO SERVICE

A COMMENCEMENT ADDRESS

I

AS I feel for a moment the wholesome dizziness that is the penalty of mounting a platform above one's fellows, and as I look down at the young faces courteously lifted for my first words, I am aware of—what shall I call it?—of an enforced collaboration; suddenly I have a vision of other rooms filled with other young men, who wait, as you do, for the first words of the commencement speaker, and at once I feel a sudden sympathy with those other speakers, who desire, as I do, to translate the occasion into wise and appropriate words. I see our various schools and colleges keeping their commencements with a single mind —the audiences all expecting the same address, and the speakers, however original, all delivering it. You expect, every graduating class expects, to be told what to do with education, now you have it; your school or college owes it to itself, you think, to confess in public the purpose for which it has trained you. I can almost hear the speakers, from ocean to ocean, responding in unison to this expectation in the graduates they face; the simultaneous eloquence is so inevitable that I can follow it almost word for word; in fact, I almost join in.

The speech they are delivering is known as the Call to Service. The substance of it is that educated men should be unselfish; that learning is a vain and dangerous luxury if it is only for ourselves; that the following of truth, the reverent touching of the hem of her garment, is not, as we may have thought, a privilege, nor is even the love of truth a virtue, until it is converted into a responsibility toward others. Few of us care to challenge this teaching. We share in the will to serve, not merely as an annual attitude, but as a year-long passion, until it becomes our one authentic motive to good living—or, if we disobey it, a witness against us, incessant and uncomfortable. No wonder that at commencement time particularly, at a moment of success and hope, the instinct of the young graduate is to hear the call to service, and the instinct of the speaker is to sound it.

Yet some of us hesitate. So long as the mind is enclosed within the happy commencement scene, the circle of well-intending graduates, affectionate parents, and earnest teachers, it is easy to say

THE CALL TO SERVICE

"Come into the world now, young man, and begin your life-long service; your good fortune, your privileges, have set you apart, but other men, alas, are also set apart by the very lack of what you have enjoyed; now bring your plenty to their want." If our thought is centered, I repeat, on those whom we call into the world, this speech comes easy, but it sticks in our throat if we begin to think of those who, we say, are in need of service. Immediately a second and profounder vision rises before us—no cheerful reaction of commencement audience and commencement speakers, but a violent opposition between the fortunate who are preparing aid and the more numerous unlucky who presumably are preparing to accept it. What confounds us is the plain fact that only those who hope to render the service have the slightest enthusiasm for it. We might well expect also some due and ardent recognition, some rising to the moment, from those about to be served. Their need, to be sure, has no such focus, no such rallying-point, as the impulse to their rescue; no commencement address puts them in mind to receive, as you graduates are stimulated to give. But their need itself, we might think, should at first prepare in them, and experience year by year confirm, a receptive and a thankful heart. Yet those about to be served are silent. If there are distinctions in silence, theirs leans less toward humility than toward defence. Those who have already been served and who now hear again the summons to their benefit, break silence by gradations of reproach. They deprecate the ministrations of the educated. They invite the physician to heal himself. They intimate hypocrisy in their would-be rescuers, who, they say, instead of equalizing men's misfortunes once for all, so that no further rescue might be needed, actually prefer to patch up life's injustices from year to year, finding a moral satisfaction in being charitable, and craving, therefore, a supply of the unfortunate to exercise that virtue on.

These criticisms, it seems to me, have too much truth in them. They throw us back upon our conscience, and force us to examine the motives with which we call others to service or answer the call ourselves. Is service truly a rescue or a profession? Do we hope to cure our neighbor's misfortune or to live by it? Nothing could be more reasonable than that service should be judged by its value to the served, yet too often we practise this unselfishness as it were for our own good; we obey the call to service as an invitation to a salutary exercise of the soul. When the disturbing vision rises before us of half the race in need, and of the other half eager to help, we must withhold approval till we ask the eager helpers, "Do you look on the unfortunate as on your brothers, in temporary distress, or do you see in them objects of charity? Do you think your function is to serve, and their function is to be served? If by a miracle they should get on their feet, would you have lost your career?"

II

If these questions seem rhetorical and strained, let me put them in other terms to several of you who presumably desire to be in the truest sense serviceable. My object, frankly, is to show that the life of service is often exploited in such a way as to come fairly within the range of criticism, and that the men who sound the call to service nowadays and those who respond to it have often no right conception of what is serviceable. I should like to indicate what are the signs of true service and what are the signs of something else that masquerades in its name.

Some of you, doubtless, have decided to enter the Church. There was a time when the call to service was identical with a call to enter the religious life. Religion, the oldest, was once the broadest avenue to good works, so broad that for centuries it included those two other main paths, now become quite secular— science and education; and with science and education it still provides the main opportunities for ministering to the soul, the body, and the mind of our fellows. Those of you, then, who contemplate the religious life, ought to be furnished out of antiquity with a definition of the service you would render; you ought to know the nature of the benefit the layman comes to religion for, and how to assist him to that benefit.

Perhaps you do not agree with me that you ought to know all this; perhaps, having felt a call to the ministry, you think the call justifies itself. As I speak, I see once more that ominous gulf between the server and the served. On one side I see you priests-to-be, loving your historical church, or your theology, or your revealed truth—loving, that is, certain gifts of God which you think you can prepare for by study, and receive by heavenly grace, and by your faithfulness transmit unimpaired to others after you; and your loyalty to theology or church or revelation you conceive to be service. On the other side of the gulf I see men waiting for real service at the hands of the Church, and not getting it. If there is hostility in the world to religion *per se*, at least that is not what I am talking about; I speak solely of those optimistic veterans in the pews who still expect the service of religion from the new arrival just out of the divinity school.

They have a pretty clear notion as to what religion promises, and they grow impatient for the promise to be kept. Religion promises, in the old words, a more abundant life, an immediate as well as a distant benefit, an enjoyment to be entered upon in this present world. It would provide at once an exercise to develop the spiritual faculties we now have into powers we but faintly imagine. "More abundant life," to the religious-minded, is the phrasing of an old battle-hope, a more than ancient faith in his own sufficiency to approach God, which individual man, in this sense forever

Puritan, has never entirely let go. Even when the priest in his primitive function stood between the people and their deity, mediating by virtue of his superior gifts and training, the savage in his fear still had glimpses of a time when each heart should perform to God its vows and sacrifices, consecrated by the mere sharing in human life. "I will make him a nation of priests," promised Jehovah to Israel. The program of religion, therefore, is not to do away with the priest, but to bestow the priestly character more abundantly upon all men.

Must I qualify my words, and say that this is only the layman's program of religion? It seems to be different from the program of the loyal priest. He hopes to perpetuate his office for the good of more and more laymen; the layman hopes that the distinction between priest and layman will disappear. The priest looks upon his office as destined to serve perpetually, and upon the layman, therefore, as destined to be perpetually an object of service; but the layman hopes to need service less and less. How very disconcerting it would be for the Church, as it is at present organized, if all the laymen should become, in the truest sense, priests. Even if we grant that the organization conforms at present to a situation, yet we detect no wish on its part that the situation should be changed. In every denomination there seems to be a tendency to widen the gulf between priest and layman, honoring the first without ennobling the second. The very devotion which is the warrant of true religion, bids the layman look up, as to a higher order of being, to the holder of the priestly office. But when a man begins as it were to cherish holiness in another's

life rather than in his own, the mischief
is done; religion then robs him of the
very thing it promises to give. If we
cannot find the illustrations close at hand,
the book of history opens at the very
places. Whenever the priesthood has
been exalted as a separate ideal of goodness or of wisdom, some integrity, some
consecration, has been taken away from
common men. In so-called Puritan moments, when the priesthood has been
least remote, the conduct of the average
man has been most nobly severe; but
where the distinctive holiness of the
priest has been most devotedly cherished,
the average man has needed a system of
pardons and indulgences. No doubt the
priests were holy, and were eager to
serve mankind, but was it service that
they actually conferred? It appears that
no man can be holy for his neighbors;
or if he persuades them to submit to the

experiment, the little holiness they have is taken away.

Perhaps you have not thought of the religious life as involving these problems. "Going into the ministry" has perhaps meant to you simply a process by which you dreamt of getting a parish to work in and people to serve. Yet even in the smallest parish the division I speak of, the opposition between priest and layman, between the serving and the served, will be awaiting you. Do you dream of a congregation to help? Your congregation dream of rising beyond need of help. Do you expect to be consecrated above the layman? The layman, who nowadays has a dialectic of his own, will ask how your consecration manifests itself. If you explain that your superiority is not in you but in your office, he will press you to explain why the office, even if sacred, is necessary; he will ask

whether a system of superiorities and in-
feriorities is vital to the religious life
and whether, if all men were equally
sanctified, the religious life would cease.

You understand that this is but a
figure of speech. The layman will not
argue with you in this fashion; he will
stay away from your church on Sunday
and avoid your society during the week.
If empty pews mean anything, he is
resolved to escape your benefits, but for
old time's sake he prefers not to quarrel
with the minister. With religion he still
has no quarrel, but the Church seems to
him actually irreligious—well-organized,
yes, well-meaning and well-behaved, even
indefatigable in distributing warm clothes
and wholesome food to the needy, yet
also in spite of her gifts increasingly remote, strangely indisposed or incom-
petent to share or impart the religious
spirit. No wonder that, since it is

spiritual development he craves, he will give his allegiance to other organizations than the Church. He sees that to join a parish for love of God comes to practically the same thing as joining it for love of the priest, to whose credit in a worldly sense an increase in the congregation is reckoned; he sees that against any criticism from the congregation the priest can and often does assert the authority of his office; he sees that though attendance at church will be counted as approval of the particular minister in charge, absence from church will be diagnosed as hostility to religion; and rather than accept the service of religion on terms so compromising to his self-respect, he retires from the field and cultivates indifference. From this mood he is roused only when a loud call to his rescue excites his wrath. The reform, he thinks, should begin elsewhere.

THE CALL TO SERVICE

III

I have been speaking to those of you who, in love of service, may think of entering the ministry, and my purpose has been to describe that gulf between your good intentions and the real needs of those whom you may have thought of as destined to be served. Yet others of you, I am aware, may not be stirred to repentance by the picture I have drawn; you may indeed be far from displeased by it. Perhaps you have left religion behind you, as an old-fashioned preoccupation of your grandmothers, and whatever seems to be a criticism of it will confirm your complacency at having left it behind. You also are in love with service, but it is the call of science that you hear—real service, as you would say, without superstition or humbug.

THE CALL TO SERVICE

Science does call you to a service of her own, but her program is perhaps less original than you think. Like religion, she would teach you an attitude of mind, an intimate approach to the universe. Like religion, science also urges you to good works; but whereas the rewards of religion are often indirect or deferred, science can appeal to your selfishness by showing an immediate as well as a remote profit. In this smaller, practical office science might be expected even to surpass the service of religion, telling you how to make yourselves immune to disease, how to regulate your diet, how to choose your dress, how to keep the streets clean, how to secure sanitation. Science has far larger and more difficult things to teach, principles and prospects of which these matters are the merest incidents; but out of her exuberant joy of service she freely bestows these simple aids toward a more abundant life.

Yet you can no more be scientific for your neighbors than you can be holy for them. If you persuade them to submit to the experiment, they will lose what little intelligence they had. Do we not see that the average man is more and more disposed to honor a few scientists, superstitiously exalting their skill into a kind of magic, and relying less and less upon himself? For every service science has rendered, some common intelligence has been taken away. She gave us the barometer, and we ceased to be weather-wise; the almanac, and we forgot the stars. If this service from without left us free to apply our knowledge in other fields, there might be a compensation for the intelligence that has been taken away. But with intelligence departs the willingness even to be intelligently served, and

just as religion falls back upon threats of
hell, so at last science calls in the police.
If my house is ventilated and sanitary,
it is not because science has made me
intelligent, but because the expert to
whom I have delegated my intelligence is
now applying it on my behalf, with or
without my consent. When my fire-
escape was cast in the foundry, perhaps
for the rescue of my life some day, they
fixed in the mold a threat to fine me ten
dollars, if ever I should block it up.

However we may condemn the result,
the intention to serve us is unmistakable.
But science is strangely inconsistent.
Having assumed the place of our intelligence, she develops what seems to be a
startling indifference to our welfare. At
times she surpasses the worst that has
been charged against religion in the disposition to fall in love with her own
image. Since the middle of the nine-

teenth century, men at her invitation
have contemplated their unsavory beginning and the myriad processes by
which they are supposed to have escaped
from it. They have not been greatly
edified; kinship with the monkey, if
true, is uninspiring. Into what nobler
relations are we to enter? Science does
not reply. The excuse is that science is
collecting facts, or perfecting methods,
or at best is occupied in remedial work,
in solving problems of disease and in reducing the discomforts of life. Service
so vast and so humane cannot be over-
valued. Yet even in the region of this
service, is not science frittering itself
away upon methods, instead of setting
before us the end? And is it possible to
estimate the value of the method, until
we know the end? One scientist tells
us, as a matter of fact, that our best days
are over at forty. Much of the informa-

tion which science imparts is as cheerful as that. Another tells us how to prolong life, by drinking sour milk. But if the first doctor is right and our heyday is over at forty, why should we wish to grow old? Our true benefactor would tell us how long we ought to wish to live. Or even when science is not so blind, it often sins by applying itself to an end it knows to be wrong. It invents vehicles of constantly greater speed, though it assures us that such acceleration is the ruin of our nerves. It invents methods of killing people, and means of protecting them, though it persuades us at the same time —as if we needed persuasion!—that war is an awkward way of serving mankind.

Those of you who heard with complacence my criticism of religion ought not to protest if I bring the same judgment to bear on science. Indeed there is a fine irony in substituting the service of science for the service of religion as a target for the fault-finder; for science, which began by pointing out the insufficiencies of religion, and gradually usurped religion's place in this matter of serving mankind, has also, it may be, taken to herself some of the frailties she once condemned. Between you and those whom you would serve through science the same gulf lies as between the priests and those they would benefit. The protest against science is not yet so loud, I grant you, as that against religion, but it is the same in kind, and it is growing. Scientists are as eager to do our thinking for us as ever the Church has been, they are just as ready to use force to make effective the truth as they see it, and they keep their scientific spirit to themselves as effectively as the priests keep their priesthood. They look upon themselves as a caste, and in the name of science

they presume to dogmatise outside of
their field, exactly as the priests once
did. We, meanwhile, as profoundly de-
sirous of magic as primitive man ever
was, wait with awe upon the word of
these latest magicians, or begin to grum-
ble because they do not let us into the
secret. We grow rich, it appears, in
the results of science, but poor in its
spirit. If the symptoms of this un-
healthy condition were found only in the
man in the street, there would be less
need to worry, for that mythical person
is by definition the first to get hold of
applied results and the last to be interested in principles. But the criticism
is justified in the places where science is
avowedly engaged in handing on her
torch—in your college, for example, where
almost all of you studied the sciences and
almost none of you was suspected by
anybody of being scientific. The technic

of the laboratory instruments appealed
to you exactly as does the management
of a motor-car or the handling of a shot-
gun; most young men like to use a
machine and to get mechanical results.
But as to learning the insatiable love of
truth, the precise observation and the
inexorable deduction which are essential
in the scientist, you probably have not
even made a beginning.

IV

I can imagine that some of you will
be as little troubled by the insufficiency of
science as by the shortcomings of religion; you have heard the call to service,
but you understand it as a call to teach.
Observing that I am by profession a
teacher, you probably think that I have
saved up education for the end of my
discourse as a happy contrast to those

other ways of serving. The call to
service does indeed seem to be a summons to inquiry, whether of religion or
science or any other region of faith or
experience, and the life of inquiry might
seem to be the life of a college professor.
The college is supposed to be a place of
precious leisure, in which truth may be
sought without distraction. It is not
directly practical nor serviceable; it is
the gymnasium rather than the arena of
the spirit. As its name implies, it is a
collection of diverse minds and natures,
strengthening their noblest impulses and
their finest knowledge by a communal
sharing. Into this charged atmosphere
of the spirit a student enters, to learn his
capacities and to develop them, as his
teachers develop theirs, by this high
traffic of soul and soul. The service
which the college can render is to keep the
atmosphere properly charged—to see that

there are enough teachers and enough students, so that this interchange of character may be complete. The ideal is a byword—"Mark Hopkins on one end of a log and a boy on the other."

The log, of course, is not necessary. It is only a convenience. But unfortunately the college is seized with that spirit of service which looks for quick results. Neither Mark Hopkins nor the boy can be organized and administered to serve any very immediate popular demand; it is the log, therefore, that the colleges have organized and elaborated. With the sincerest desire to be of service to the greatest number—if possible, to all who present themselves—they have extended the log till some of the boys are almost out of earshot of Mark Hopkins, and for weak backs they have inserted a few bolsters. How narrow and unsympathetic sounds an extract from the report to the trustees of Columbia College in 1810 on the state of instruction in that institution—"Your committee cannot for a moment suppose that it is the intention of the Board to try that most fruitless and mischievous experiment—the experiment of educating either the naturally stupid or the incurably idle."

In justice to the modern educator who does not admit the existence of any such class as the naturally stupid or the incurably idle, be it said that he lives up to his ideal of service, even to the forfeiture of that leisurely investigation and contemplation of truth which is the prime delight of the scholar. The log has not been easy to organize. The college professor has had to manipulate embarrassing entrance requirements, and make the curriculum pliable, and serve as preceptor to the near-idle and as adviser to the near-stupid; nay, having evolved this

system of dependence in intellectual
things, he has carried it, in the spirit of
service, into the amusements of the
students, until he acts as director of
their sports and treasurer of their gate
receipts and sponsor of their business
contracts. All this takes time. In more
leisurely days the scholar would come
from his meditations upon great truths
like the prophet from Sinai, with the
skin of his face shining. Now from a
conference with student managers or
from investigating the eligibility of the
football captain he returns with that
nervous step, that fretful eye, that
palpable collapse of spirit, which announce to his sympathetic colleagues,
"I have served."

Yet he would still have his reward,
did his labors ennoble the served, or con-
fer upon them a more abundant life.
That the effect is otherwise might be

prophesied from a certain complacency
in his sacrifice. If he looks down to those
he serves, if the angle of his condescen-
sion is to himself the warrant of his well-
doing, if football or the college dramatics
be not really his career, but only an
excuse for demonstrating to the young-
sters that he can still revisit their point
of view—then he has robbed them of
what it is his profession to give; robbed
them not simply in their greater dependence, in their lessening enthusiasm
and ability to conduct their own affairs, but far more tragically in the de-
feat of their right to live in the presence,
and profit by the inspiration, of a
scholar who follows with his whole heart
the great quest of truth. Whether or
not it is the students' duty to study, it is
their right to behold the scholar at his
work, and to imitate him; for it is by
comradeship and imitation that they

share the teacher's life. But if the
teacher keeps his scholarship out of the
comradeship and the life which they
share; if he manages his days as though
scholarship were a solace of the leisure
to be earned by service, or a hoarded
treasure not to be rashly displayed—he
will no more make others scholarly than
a priest who conceals his holiness will
make others holy, or a scientist who does
not live his science will make others
scientific.

V

It would be wrong to let you think
that by entering any great profession,
even my own, you will automatically
enter the life of genuine service. With
teaching, with science, with religion, I
have no quarrel; I long ago gave my
allegiance to all three, and it is from

noble priests and scholars and teachers
that I have drawn the ideals here set
forth. But while human nature remains
what it is, there is a great temptation to
mistake immediate results for the true
ends, to impart the by-products rather
than the vital principle, to think of ourselves as conserving the torch, instead
of handing it on. The mass of mankind are good-natured enough to let us
treat them for a certain length of time as
objects of charity, as destined to be
served, but there is an end to their good
nature. In religion this conclusion has
already shown itself; in science and in
education the writing is on the wall.
For that reason I hesitated to call you
to service, lest you should understand
the summons only in the familiar way,
and by your enthusiasm should make
the gulf wider between your ideals
and your fellow-men. But to be truly

serviceable is our loftiest ambition. The
service we dream of is such education,
such religion, such science, as will increase
in all men the abundance of life. The
method we dream of is such an illustration
of religion or science or scholarship in
our own lives as will increase in others a
hunger for the same spiritual sustenance.
To make this illustration, we must first
cultivate religion or science or scholarship in ourselves.

This is the statement of the call to
service which I have been approaching
slowly and with care, for to the generous-
hearted it is on first acquaintance a hard
saying. Seek truth or seek goodness for
yourselves, if you wish others to have it.
If you rise to your own stature, you will
thereby perform all the service you
could desire—you will help others to rise.
Doubtless some of your neighbors will
think you selfish. Doubtless the man

who buried his talent in a napkin was
answering the call to service elsewhere.
The sacrifice was his own concern, but
the service so rendered must have been
for the served also a lessening of spiritual
wealth. True service lessens nothing.
Not that the teacher should waste himself in the enterprises of boyhood, but
that even boys should fall in love with
the enterprise of truth; not that the
scientist should become a commodity-
monger, but that all men should enjoy
the high commodity of the scientific
spirit; not that the priest should be
secularized, but that by a race-wide consecration man should become a nation of
priests—this is the end of true service.
For this we must be patient and with
becoming care make ourselves ready; it
is required of us only that we be produc-
tive of good at last. For a thousand
years of inspiration to unnumbered men,

how brief an investment are the forty
years, or fifty, of the scholar's seclusion,
the saint's discipline! Meanwhile the
humble apprentice, so he be faithful, is
even at the moment serviceable; for
none of us can withdraw himself so far,
but he will be still a ganglion of inspiration for all whose fate, by accident or kinship, is bound with his. We cannot too
greatly desire to bring our fellows to the
truth, but we may underestimate their
own desire for it. When we ourselves
seek it, every man who feels our contact
will go with us.

This is the true call to service—not,
"The world is waiting for you—come and
help it"; but, "Are you fit to serve?
Do you know how to live your own
life? Either religion or science may be
for you the City of God. If the ram-
parts need rebuilding, take counsel of
those ancient men who after long cap-

tivity raised again the walls of Jerusa-
lem. Every man built in front of his
own house."

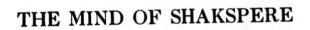

THE MIND OF SHAKSPERE

THE MIND OF SHAKSPERE

I

IN a recent guide-book to Shakspere occur certain questions intended to promote critical faculty in the student. "What amount of time," asks the writer, examining *A Midsummer Night's Dream*, "is covered by the entire action, according to the direction given at the beginning of the play? Show by references the time-scheme which seems to you to be actually followed." The student is here expected to perceive a discrepancy. Then, continues the questioner, "Why did Shakspere allow this discrepancy to remain in the play?" Again, "Note cases of *stichomythia*, or dialogue in which each

speech consists of a single line. Is it
effective in each case, or does it seem
artificial?" And finally, "For what different purposes, in this play, does Shakspere seem to use blank verse, five-accent
rimed lines, four-accent rime, and prose?"

As we read these questions and others
like them, beyond a doubt helpful toward
a serious weighing of Shakspere's genius,
they suggest perhaps a larger question
which from time to time has troubled us
all, and for which some of us have not
heard the sufficient answer. They suggest the question of Shakspere's mind.
They bid us ask once more, is his art the
result of intention, or is there another
explanation of it; and if there is another
explanation, does this sort of catechism
make allowance for it? In these familiar
phases,—"why did Shakspere allow,"
"for what purpose does Shakspere seem
to use,"—in this echo of the formulas

most teachers unconsciously lean to, there
is an implication which not a few lovers
of poetry may care to challenge. Admit-
ting that all the manifestations of genius
are proper subjects for minute study, we
may yet be fearful of the missteps of
scholarship in the uncertain field of art;
we may doubt whether any phrase which
even slightly emphasizes the design and
intention of the great poet's craft, does
not follow as an unrecorded premise the
critic's knowledge of his own rather than
of Shakspere's mind.

For we cannot too often recall that
this man's fame, moving up through
heavens of misty or pedantic adoration,
has obligingly modified itself to the scope
of the beholding eye. Whatever rest his
curse procured for his bones, we have
made chameleon work of his reputation.
We have thought of him with Ben Jonson
as an improviser, or with Milton as

fancy's child, or with Arnold as a solitary peak, lifting above us inscrutable, unscanned. Nothing in this tradition would prohibit one more guess at Shakspere's mind. Yet in the newest explanation there will be a few things in common with those that went before. From the beginning the world has felt the naturalness of this well-poised genuis; he never dwelt apart, starlike. No explanation will satisfy us which does not make Shakspere's mind a thing of nature—even a normal thing, in kind if not in degree. From the beginning the world has acknowledged the comprehensiveness of his imagination; at times so slight a barrier of visible art divides the life he saw from his representation of it, that life itself appears the medium of his thought. No explanation of his mind will satisfy us which does not make reasonable this godlike grasp upon experience. From the beginning also there has been an adverse opinion of Shakspere's craft; if we are to believe the extreme criticism of him, he never revised his work, he was sometimes careless of his grammar, he was sometimes all but indifferent to dramatic structure. Though the volume of his fame has more or less overwhelmed all fault-finding, no sincere attempt to explain his mind will neglect to bring even the rumor of his defects to a final account.

The desirable explanation, therefore, will answer the question of his naturalness, the question of his comprehensiveness, the question of his imperfections. The well-known attempts to understand this elusive intellect have, however, usually busied themselves with only one or two of these aspects. Such a partial solution is in Hartley Coleridge's beautiful sonnet:

THE MIND OF SHAKSPERE

"Like that Ark,
Which in its sacred hold uplifted high,
O'er the drowned hills, the human family,
And stock reserved of every living kind,
So in the compass of the single mind
The seeds and pregnant forms in essence lie
That make all worlds. Great Poet, 'twas thy art
To know thyself, and in thyself to be
Whate'er love, hate, ambition, destiny,
Or the firm, fatal purpose of the heart
Can make of man."

Helpful as the simile is, it illuminates only the comprehensiveness of Shakspere's mind; it ignores the shortcomings of his workmanship and the limitations of his thought; it is inconsistent with perhaps any theory of his apparently natural inspiration. True, all men observe, not the world outside, but themselves—since what they see is at best only their conception of what they see; with this interpretation Shakspere's art may be said to consist solely in his observation of himself. Yet this would be

to spin too fine Coleridge's already subtle
thought. His meaning is clear enough;
he would stress Shakspere's independence
of knowledge gained by experience; this
most precious intellect was freighted once
for all with the infinite fortunes and aspirations of the race, and—to exaggerate
slightly—neither study nor thought nor
travel nor age could add one little weight
of knowledge. A mind so described is
not the normal mind, as we know it, and
in the description is no place for that
flavor of contact, that smack of immediate experience, which is the first
mark of Shaksperian thought.

Most of the criticism of our century,
even of our own day, would explain
Shakspere's comprehensiveness at the
cost of his naturalness. German philosophy in the early years and German
scholarship later have tried to establish
a sort of standard of omniscience, against

which the poet's faults if perceived at
all are measured as lapses from his true
self. From Germany, though he denied
it, the elder Coleridge learned to deal
with Shakspere as with a god, whose
mind was of a higher order than ours,
yet might with labor be dimly learned;
whose clearest utterance hinted at divine
plans not in our fate to conceive, but
only to admire; whose occasional vacu-
ities meant no more than that the god
perchance was sleeping or on a journey.
"A nature humanized," Coleridge pictures Shakspere, "a genial understanding
directing self-consciously a power and an
implicit wisdom deeper even than our
consciousness." Again, echoing the theme
of his son's verses, he gives us this conception of a meditating, Coleridgean
Shakspere—"The body and substance
of his works came out of the depths of
his own oceanic mind; his observation

THE MIND OF SHAKSPERE

and reading, which was considerable, supplied him with the draperies of his figures." And again, "He was not only a great poet, but a great philosopher."

No more significant but probably better known is that passage in which Hazlitt subtilizes about the mind of Shakspere, saying nothing new, perhaps, but setting an example in his phrase for the manner of question we noticed in the student's guide-book. "The striking peculiarity of Shakspere's mind," he says, "was its generic quality, its power of communication with all other minds, so that it contained a universe of thought and feeling within itself, and had no one peculiar bias or exclusive excellence more than another. He was just like any other man, but that he was like all other men. He not only had in himself the germs of every faculty and feeling, but he could follow them by anticipation, in-

tuitively, into all their conceivable rami-
fications, through every change of fortune, or conflict of passion, or turn of
thought. . . . He turned the globe round
for his amusement, and surveyed the
generations of men, and the individuals
as they passed, with their different con-
cerns, passions, follies, vices, virtues,
actions, and motives—as well those that
they knew, as those that they did not
know or acknowledge to themselves."

Through this rhapsody how shall we
approach the man Shakspere with human
faults of speech and conduct; or how
shall we see the roots of his genius in any
faculty that is ours?

This school of criticism might be called
the philosophical adoration of Shakspere.
In the soberer end of the nineteenth century we have had the scholarly adoration,
a milder but no less devoted flame, as
befits much telling of syllables and

matching of texts. To make the account somewhat brief—those who have studied the matter know that the chief furnishings of Shakspere's lodgings and of his theatres must have been the shelves crowded with his sources. Where an earlier version is not forthcoming, as in *Love's Labor's Lost*, we yet live in hope; if it be not found, at least some thesis will prove that it has been mislaid. We are supposed to know also that Shakspere was a lawyer, a doctor, an experimental psychologist, a sociologist, an aristocrat, a democrat, a moralist, a cryptic preacher of esoteric religion. To be specific, we observe, for example, that in modern society rich and idle families when they degenerate have a trick of announcing their end in one of two ways; the latest descendant sometimes reverts to the original vulgarity and common sense of the peasant who founded the line and

by dint of practice and the family fortune becomes an almost efficient, if uneconomic, hunter or sailor or farmer; or
the latest descendant inherits grace of
manner, the cumulative breeding of generations, but the exhausted stock be-
queathes him nothing more, and he is
at best a gentlemanly fool. This two-
fold degeneracy the student of society
teaches us to observe,—and lo! Sir Toby
Belch and Sir Andrew Ague-cheek. Or,
to illustrate again, the old French poets
had a definite type of lyric called the
chanson d'aubade, or dawn song—the
complement of the serenade, or evening
song. A famous example of this type,
the French scholar tells the French student, is "Hark! Hark! the lark," from
Cymbeline. One other type of dawn song,
the *chanson d'aube*, expressed the sorrow
of two lovers who must leave each other's
arms at daybreak. Among the marks of

this type are the man's anxiety not to be found by his enemies, and the woman's reckless desire to detain him if only for a moment. He tells her that already the birds of dawn are singing; she answers that he hears the birds of a darkening twilight. And of this type of French lyric there is one perfect illustration, Juliet's cry to Romeo,

"Will you begone? It is not yet near day!
It was the nightingale and not the lark."

So Shakspere is become a research scholar, poor man!

Or dare we dissent from all that this sort of criticism implies? Only two things actually known of Shakspere bear on this problem; for other aids to the understanding of his mind we should look not in books, but in life. We know that he was a man of action, a man infinitely busy with practical affairs, a man who produced several plays a year, and who could have no leisure. We know also that from the first he had a fluent gift of speech; he could say what he would, with the least possible impediment of language. But for the radical secret of his mind perhaps we should look in our own experience, if we would justify the hope that he was such a man as we are.

II

What, for instance, is the effect of his plays on us? For one thing, we understand them, as we could hardly do if they were the work of superhuman intelligence. What audience was ever puzzled by a Shakspere play? It is only the theories of his critics that perplex. Further, the plays seem to the audience to be miracles not of intellect but of observation. No doubt the poet was thoughtful; no doubt his mind brooded on life; but in his plays he gives the results of clear vision, not the results of clear thinking.

Might we not find a clue to the secret in the behavior and expression of children before they are instructed as to what they ought to think and say? Who of us cannot recall at least one of their disconcertingly apposite remarks? Their naïve pronouncements share with great poetry the double effect of echo and surprise; we who hear have felt our way towards some such idea, yet when it confronts us we are startled. For highly conventionalized people, like Tennyson's spinster, children in their talkative moods are almost demoniacal,

"a-haxin ma hawkward questions, an saayin ondecent things."

But their youthful penetration is not solely a cause of embarrassment. Sometimes it shocks us to repentance for the unnatural state of mind into which we have grown. When Mr. Brocklehurst asked little Jane Eyre what she must do in order to avoid hell fire after death, she replied, "I must keep in good health, and not die." Why not, after all? We have been educated to a less natural answer. Sometimes this penetration is the very gift of prophecy. When young William Blake was to be apprenticed to a certain painter, the boy objected, saying that the man looked as if he were to be hanged. And the man later did come to be hanged.

This faculty in childhood, which we can all illustrate for ourselves, appears to be nothing more than accurate, natural observation—an almost animal power of sight such as a fine dog or horse would have—and spontaneous, unretarded expression. As we grow older, learning to

consider our thoughts we become conventional—that is, we train ourselves to
see only what we expect to see. And
learning to consider our speech, we limit
our vocabulary; for the effect of taking
thought is to curtail, not extend, our supply of words. Because we are unsure
of many a fine word, or because we are
unsteady in its pronunciation, we ordinary grown folk will not use it; and
we hesitate to write it, forsooth, because
of the spelling. Yet what energetic
child, before he has been to school, ever
stops for a word? Will he not make one
up as he needs it, and pronounce it as
he can, and by the same guidance spell
it—very much in the way of that reckless
word-user, William Shakspere? As to
that unspoiled power to see true, some
vestiges of it we grown folk perceive
when upon meeting a stranger or seeing
a landscape we feel an instant reaction,

an impulsive judgment which craves expression, but which we stifle because we did not expect it. And a few seconds later perhaps some unconsidering person says the very thing, and wins a prompt acclaim.

Is there not a hint of Shakspere in this? To be sure, he was no child, but a mature man, educated to some extent in the knowledge of his time, if not in the profundities of modern scholarship. His associates were probably better educated than he, and his daily conference with them must have subjected his thought to a thousand influences of wisdom which we shall never be able to trace specifically among his "sources." Yet with all this maturity, can we not imagine a grown person with whom for the most part expression has remained an instantaneous reflex of experience, who sees true habitually, as we less child-like folk do occa-

sionally, and who speaks so spontaneously
that he takes no account of his utterance? He never blotted a line, if we believe Ben Jonson; and even if we do not
believe him, it is harder to prove that
Shakspere's second thought is in any of
the texts, than it is to conceive of his
mind at its best as unspoiled by intention or reconsideration, like the mind
of a child whose penetrating, unconscious
criticism of life has not yet been ruined
by blame or praise. With such a conception, the known facts of Shakspere's
life cease to be puzzling. Hawthorne
wondered that poetic genius could grow
up in the small Stratford house, where
there was no privacy. Probably Hawthorne's meditative genius could not have
grown up there, but for Shakspere's mind
there could be no happier school. At
all times and places his mental process
was normal; he needed no privacy for

penurious inspiration, but in the very heart of noisy, roistering Southwark could reflect the life that crowded in upon him; and doubtless the lack of seclusion in his father's house fostered the gift. Indeed, privacy and leisure would probably have meant starvation for his art. The fortunate conditions for the development of his energy and his naturalness, were a crowded and stirring environment and the necessity of ceaseless labor. It is no miracle that in a few years filled with distractions he produced in such rapid succession so many plays; had he enjoyed an unstimulating quiet, perhaps only by a miracle would he have produced any plays at all.

Shakspere's energy, which we assume as the prime fact in his character, is too generally conceded to call for proof. In the details of his career from the imprudent marriage and the deer-stealing to the purchase of New Place and the return to Stratford, he was a man of action fully occupied with affairs. Professor Wallace's recent contributions to our knowledge of his life in London, set him still more clearly in this light. But his writing might teach us as much without the help of the biographers. Great energy, strong interest, whether a man be very happy or very angry, results in vividness of imagination and felicity of speech. Shakspere's writing further reminds us that it is too much to expect even him to live invariably in a tense, reacting frame of mind, wherein life is observed and created with infallible energy. Many a dull and self-conscious passage—if we may be forgiven for observing them!—is witness to his relaxed moments. Yet it would not be difficult to argue that his best work was done in his busiest years. That he mingled with other men in a companionable way, without much hint that he or they thought him more than a genial, frank comrade, is no paradox, but the inevitable consequence of his interest in life and his energy; nor should we wonder that his family remembered him in the death record as a gentleman, not as the world's greatest poet. His business was to live, not to write. That we have his plays now, means only that poetry is the most enduring reaction to life. He illustrates the usually forgotten truth that the greatest poets, normal and not too conscious of themselves, are men of action. Like Dante or Milton or Scott, he responded to life in other ways than through poetry—only he set so great value on the other ways and so little on the poetry that we are forced to think him the least conscious and most naïve of artists.

THE MIND OF SHAKSPERE

If his unconscious energy illuminates
his vast accomplishment, it throws light
as well upon his narrowest limitation.
Since his genius at its typical moments
reflected life in spontaneous, uncalculat-
ing speech, no wonder that his horizon
was narrowly bounded by human birth
and death. His thought attempted no
other world, no other life, than this.
His mind could not react happily on
what could not be physically seen.
Dante's imaginings or Milton's were
therefore impossible to his temperament;
indeed, the casual questions of any
serious-minded contemporary of his as
to a future existence were to him it
seems strange and forbidding. In *Hamlet* and *Measure for Measure*, those dark
adventures in the borderland of death,
the practical wisdom of life is profound,
but the brooding upon the hereafter is
child-like, with a child's respect for angels

and devils, and a more certain dread
of ghosts and of being alone in the dark.

The other fact of Shakspere's equip-
ment which needs no proof is his gift of
language. Distinction must be made of
course between his natural endowment
and the felicitous word-play which he
shared with his contemporaries. It was
a languaged age. What Shakspere owed
to Euphuism is known to all students of
his style. The fashion of fine cadences
helped him to many a much-commen-
taried line, sounding and shallow, like

"And peace proclaims olives of endless age,"

or taught him such a flawless stretch
of song as satisfies us though we forget
the allusion—

"And the imperial votaress passed on
In maiden meditation fancy-free,"

or shorter phrases, now proverbial, like

THE MIND OF SHAKSPERE

"Sweets to the Sweet,"

"More sinned against than sinning."

In these felicities, however, Shakspere surpassed but little the other poets of his time, who improved their vocabulary and style, as we nowadays would do, by taking thought. Any one with an ordinary ear for word-music could effect some such happy combinations of sound. If he should occasionally miss the mark, so also did Shakspere; immediately before and after these quoted lines occur others far less happy. That he excelled at all in the practice of Euphuism, that he had a higher average of happy lines to his credit than others in that fashion, is proof only of his delight in language for its own sake—a delight that is common in some degree to all poets.

Even in the highly Euphuistic passages, however, with alliteration and balance and the other artifices of style, some magic word often lives with the Shaksperian vitality. Among the "w's" and the "l's" and the "k" sounds of the following most familiar lines, the verb which gives the picture has an eerie detonation, a charm that it never wore in any other employment—

> "On such a night
> Stood Dido with a willow in her hand
> Upon the wild sea bank, and *waft* her love
> To come again to Carthage."

The distinction of Shakspere's language at its best is its extraordinary vitality. Words to most men are listless things, to be combined into stationary forms of thought or color. But in the Shaksperian word there is always a certain astonishment, a new approach, whether or not the word has been familiar before—

"In the dead *vast* and middle of the night."

"Nothing of him that doth fade
But doth suffer a *sea-change*."

"Age cannot wither her, nor *custom stale*
Her infinite variety."

Does not the secret of this imaginative speech lie in the poet's clearness of vision and in his immediateness and accuracy of expression? Such words cannot be found by careful search in one's vocabulary; they are found, if at all, in the thing contemplated, when the energy of the poet's nature provides—to take a liberty with his own phrase—that the firstlings of his sight shall be the firstlings of his speech. To a degree children have this spontaneous felicity, at least as long as they keep a naïve approach to language. Until they are spoiled by self-consciousness they do not think the words—they see them, as something new and wonderful. Certain child-like ages, notably the Elizabethan, have rediscovered language, have toyed with it and manipulated it,—even distorted it; and Shakspere, the supreme child of a child-like age, when his interest was diverted from word-play to the spectacle of life, energized that life with unreflecting abandon into language curiously haphazard and uneven, but at its best a matchless symbol or incarnation of life itself.

III

The theory of Shakspere's mind which is here put forth seems to find two objections. The sonnets, which follow a contemporary fashion in a set literary form, can hardly be accounted for as the unconscious product of the naïve contemplation of life. And in the plays

there seems to be constant though uneven evidence of design, and in the later
plays especially the poet seems to speak
as a philosopher, passing conscious ver-
dicts upon life. It was this philosophical
matter that led Coleridge and his school
to see in Shakspere a profound nature.

This paper does not intend, of course,
to announce the great dramatist as a sort
of automaton, who had no sense of the
quality or purport of his work. In the
sonnets and the early plays Shakspere is
artificially self-conscious. But he is the
most uneven of great writers; even in his
artificial moments he is capable of naïve
utterance, of that penetrating truth
which is his characteristic; on the other
hand, in his noblest passages of this sort
he sometimes indulges in palpable tricks
of style or artifice of idea. Without
raising the mooted questions of the sonnets, we can agree with those many

critics who have found in them some of
Shakspere's happiest phrases; whatever
else they are, they are born of a nature
in love with fine speech. If we study
the style of the sonnets at all, however,
it is only fair to reckon with the style
of all of them—not simply to dwell
upon the most felicitous, in the habit of
the Shaksperian fanatics. At least, it is
only fair to reckon with them all if we
are to use them as indications of the
poet's mind. The series has had its fame
from a bare dozen of really splendid
sonnets, much helped by the dramatic
story which seems to be their background, and which may or may not be
autobiography. It is hard not to think
that the noblest of these poems are direct
reflections of life; yet it does not follow
that the whole story is. On the contrary, there are rather more sonnets of
an artificiality so great as to raise the

doubt whether the poet knew anything of love at all. Did the imagination that fashioned the Dark Lady, or uttered the terrible curse of lust, or the superb praise of friendship and of the "marriage of true minds," equally indulge in chop-logic? The examples are familiar. To choose one—

"If I love thee, my loss is my love's gain,
And losing her, my friend hath found that loss;
Both find each other, and I lose both twain,
And both for my sake lay on me this cross.
But here's the joy; my friend and I are one;
Sweet flattery! Then she loves but me alone."

Or the whole of the following sonnet, with its amazing artifice—

"When most I wink, then do mine eyes best see,
For all the day they view things unrespected;
But when I sleep, in dreams they look on thee,
And darkly bright are bright in dark directed.
Then thou, whose shadow shadows doth make
bright,
How would thy shadow's form form happy show

To the clear day with thy much clearer light,
When to unseeing eyes thy shade shines so!
How would, I say, mine eyes be blessed made
By looking on thee in the living day,
When in dead night thy fair imperfect shade
Through heavy sleep on sightless eyes doth
    stay!
All days are nights to see till I see thee,
And nights bright days when dreams do show
    thee me."

If this sort of writing indicates anything of the writer's mind, it tells us that he was practising the devices of style with great ingenuity. The human experience contained in the poem, however, is hardly what his admirers would like to call Shaksperian. Nor does it aid them greatly to say that here Shakspere was learning his craft. What craft? The use of language? Perhaps,—though he used language less and less often in this fashion. But how is this sort of hair-splitting a training for his knowledge of life? What is the connection between

these lines and Hamlet's words with
Horatio—

"Has this fellow no feeling of his business, that
   he sings at grave-making?
   "*Horatio.* Custom hath made it in him a
      property of easiness.
   "*Hamlet.* 'Tis e'en so: the hand of little
      employment hath the daintier sense."

Or if the sonnets and early plays of
Shakspere were a training for his art,
how comes it that even in the mature
plays he slips into unfinished and un-
distinguished passages? It is usual to
say that in the later work his thought
overbalanced his speech, at times to the
confusion of both; but it would be easier
to suppose that throughout his life his
moments of energetic vision alternated
with very ordinary states of consciousness, and that he had little sense of the
value of one condition over the other.
The sonnets clearly echo older plots and

older sonnet series. It is impossible
to prove them autobiographical as a
whole. Yet it is just as difficult to deny
the similitude of personal experience in
the great sonnets. Shakspere followed
the sonnet fashion, as he followed other
fashions, doing only what others had
done, but doing it better, with more
energy; and in the process he lights up
unexpected and amazing areas of truth.

To say that in his later plays the
thought overbalances the language, is to
raise the main question as to whether
Shakspere was a thinker at all. According to the theory of his mind here advanced, he was not. Except for his
characteristic moments in which he
flashes life into words, he is curiously
conventional and timid. Though he followed the daring Marlowe and was the
contemporary of Bacon, he never ven-
tured out of the most conservative, even

non-committal, attitudes toward religion and learning and the established professions. The endings of many of his plays and the initial circumstances of others, completely ignore the logic of the plot and of the characters; he is content that the scene should open and close upon artificial situations, but while the story is in motion he vitalizes it with his naïve energy. If he is the greatest of world-dramatists, is he not also the playwright who has taught least to posterity? He did with supreme excellence what had been done before him, but added practically nothing to the craft of the theatre; the modern dramatist goes to other men for technical instruction.

If Shakspere was a thinker, he must have accepted the conclusions of his own wisdom; if he did not know when he uttered wisdom, he was hardly a thinker. It is easier to take the latter conclusion,

though the admiring school have implied
that Shakspere knew his own profundity,
but carried the secret to his grave. The
difficulty with that explanation is that
it makes Shakspere practically omniscient. The Baconian heresy and other
attempts to explain him, have been
attempts to explain the author that
Coleridge and the Germans found in the
plays. Foolish as is the doctrine that
Bacon could write and produce these
dramas and have the secret kept for
two centuries, it is really wiser than the
belief that Shakspere could have been
consciously omniscient, and yet keep the
secret to himself—nay, even write a great
many shallow things to hide the fact.

To be sure, almost every phase of
earthly life is glanced at in the plays.
Yet this does not prove that Shakspere
thought about any of them; he merely
observed them. For example, the fa-

vorite memory of our first acquaintance
with political economy is that question
about what sort of society we would
establish if cast upon a desert island. In
The Tempest, when the King of Naples
and his courtiers find themselves on what
they think is a deserted island, they
argue this very question. Says Gonzalo,

"Had I plantation of this very isle, my lord—
     .   .   .   .   .   .
I' the commonwealth I would by contraries
Execute all things; for no kind of traffic
Would I admit; no name of magistrate;
Letters should not be known; riches, poverty,
And use of service, none; contract, succession,
Bourn, bound of land, tilth, vineyard, none;
No use of metal, corn, or wine or oil;
No occupation; all men idle, all;
     .   .   .   .   .   .
All things in common nature should produce
Without sweat or endeavor; treason, felony,
Sword, pike, knife, gun, or need of any engine,
Would I not have; but nature should bring
     forth,
Of its own kind, all foison, all abundance,
To feed my innocent people."

Now are we to believe that Shakspere here anticipates and pokes fun at the speculations of political economy, or that having this group of men upon a desert island he perceives the possibilities of the speculation, and puts into Gonzalo's mouth a translation of words used with another reference by Montaigne?

So with those curious coincidences which are strewn through the dramas. The poet has a trick—say some critics— of putting into the first words of the leading persons a clue to their characters. When Romeo says, "Is the day then so young," we are to see in him the embodiment of youth. It is easy enough to find marvels of this sort in Shakspere— perhaps in every poet. The themes of this same play of *Romeo and Juliet* may be said to be the conflict of Youth with Age—Age having forgotten what young love is like; and also the conflict of

Love with Hate—Hate being expressed
in the feud, which in turn is incarnate in
Tybalt. It is easy enough for us to
think of the story in these terms, but
did Shakspere so think of it while writing
it? and did he summarize the themes
intentionally in a passage at the end of
Act I? Capulet speaks first, doubtless
representing Age—

"Nay, sit, nay, sit, good cousin Capulet,
For you and I are past our dancing days:
How long is't now since last yourself and I
Were in a mask?

Second Capulet. By'r lady, thirty years.
Cap. What, man! 'tis not so much, 'tis not so
　　much:
'Tis since the nuptial of Lucentio,
Come pentecost as quickly as it will,
Some five and twenty years: and then we masked.
Sec. Cap. 'Tis more, 'tis more: his son is elder,
　　sir;
His son is thirty.
Cap.　　　　　　Will you tell me that?
His son was but a ward two years ago."

Immediately Romeo speaks, representing Youth and Love—

"What lady is that, which doth enrich the hand
Of yonder knight?
    Serving-man. I know not, sir.
    Rom. O, she doth teach the torches to burn
        bright!
It seems she hangs upon the cheek of night
Like a rich jewel in an Ethiope's ear;
Beauty too rich for use, for earth too dear!
So shows a snowy dove trooping with crows,
As yonder lady o'er her fellows shows.
The measure done, I'll watch her place of stand,
And, touching hers, make blessed my rude hand.
Did my heart love till now? forswear it, sight!
For I ne'er saw true beauty till this night."

Now enters Tybalt, who personifies the last theme, Hate—

"This, by his voice, should be a Montague.
Fetch me my rapier, boy."

It makes all the difference whether we believe that Shakspere consciously inserted these designs or patterns in his work, or that they are there because they

are in life, and the poet, reflecting life,
mirrored more than he knew. The *chanson d'aube* and the *aubade* are in old
French literature, but Shakspere never
found them there; he found them, where
the old French poets found them, in a
dramatic situation of real life. Hamlet
was the victim of heredity; the conflict
of the vacillating mother and of the
downright father was in him; yet Shakspere only perceived in life what we have
perceived there also and have learned
to call heredity. When Macbeth says
that he has murdered sleep, and we
trace through the play the remorseful
sleeplessness which finally drives Lady
Macbeth to suicide, we may call Shakspere a criminal psychologist if we choose,
but he only observed what we have
classified. He saw that we are such
stuff as dreams are made of, but he
probably would not have agreed with

Bishop Berkeley. These designs in Shakspere are true and recognizable, but they are coincidences, like the Dipper in the heavens; we cannot think that a supreme intelligence marshalled planets and stars to illustrate a kitchen utensil.

IV

This view of Shakspere may seem to belittle him, as reducing his work to the improvisations of a child. The kingdom of heaven was once thought to be for aristocracy of intellect, and some of us think as much of the kingdom of poetry; but there is good authority for believing that they are both open to the imaginative, to those who can be unconscious of self as little children. Great intellect alone cannot force its way in, and it is the part of intelligence to recognize that fact. There is, of course, no reason

why great intellect and great poetic
faculty—the ability to reason and the
ability to see and feel and speak—should
not meet in the same person. They did
so meet in Sophocles and in Euripides.
But it seems that they did not so meet
in Shakspere, and perhaps it is only a
wilful praise of the poet of our own
tongue that would call him, on the whole,
the equal of the Greek dramatists.

If we make an intelligent distinction,
however, between logical or analytical
power and the poetic gift, then this
theory of Shakspere's naïve mind is not
without hope for a richer conception of
the nature of poetry. Shakspere's critics have measured themselves in their
measure of him. Milton, who prayed
that his own lips might be touched with
fire from off the sacred altar, beheld in
the dramatist a secular, somewhat secondary, prophet of the same ineffable

inspiration. Coleridge, philosopher and dreamer, never a man of action, saw in Shakspere a Prospero, a magician, controlling the ends of life by study and forethought. Arnold, the self-reliant, somewhat estranged servant of culture, expecting or desiring from men neither comprehension nor contact, imaged the poet in the unattainable, unguessed-at height. And if with another attitude we perceive in the mind of Shakspere only the most fortunate occurrence of qualities common to all men—only the eye to see, the heart to feel, the tongue to speak, and the absence of that overcaution which ceases to live when it stops to think—may it not be that our age, with all its sophistication, consciously aspires to the immediateness and the simplicity of life, and to that poetry which is not the accomplishment but the essence of life?

MAGIC AND WONDER IN LITERATURE

MAGIC AND WONDER IN
LITERATURE

I

WIDELY as we all differ in knowledge and in opinions, one general account of life we are supposed as educated men to accept. We are supposed to agree that we live in a universe of order; that every effect, though to us unexplained, has proceeded from a cause, and that the same causes operate faithfully at all times. If it is the outward world that engages us, we are supposed to perceive that the stars which seem to wander, nevertheless are true to their courses; that no wind bloweth where it listeth, for we do know whence

it comes and whither it goes; that the
flood and the earthquake, once monsters
of caprice, are now phenomena of obedi-
ence; that even chance has its law. If we
look inward upon our reason, our emotions, our instincts, we are supposed to see
that the mind, like other instruments, can
be controlled, and that its relation to the
outer world is so much the same in all
men that we can speak of colors or of
sounds, can frame a syllogism, express a
desire, distinguish between the abstract
and the concrete, and be understood.
Finally, if our concern is with morals,
we are supposed to conclude that since
ideas and emotions are an established cur-
rency among men, personality must be
something constant and reliable. Knowing a man's mind and his character,
we can predict that in a given situation he will think thus and behave so
and so; and conversely, from the opinions

uttered or the conduct adopted in a given situation, we can infer the character of a stranger. It seems that law of one kind or another is the condition on which we live, and that we illustrate as superb a logic as do the planets above us.

Whether or not there are dissenters from this account of the universe, at least we may fairly say that this account is the basis of most thinking to-day. It is accepted, of course, with humility. Even within the limits of our powers, we have as yet gained far less control of experience than our intellectual self-respect demands. We still blunder through life as though we did not know that the great game must be played according to the rules. But at least we admit that there are rules, and that when man has learned them, he will find the game much easier and happier to play. Having made this admission, how-

ever, it is to be feared that we forget
our humility and become self-satisfied.
This orderly definition of the universe, we
reflect, is something of an achievement,
and we assume that it is peculiarly our
own. The Greeks, to be sure, and a few
others, seem to have had the idea, but
this only shows, as we say, how modern
the Greeks were. Primitive man in
general, we are quite certain, preferred
mystery to order, refused to recognize
the most obvious causes, and rarely did
a thing directly if by indirection he
could get it done more awkwardly.
Here again we are somewhat checked
when the archæologist comes upon some
primitive implement strangely effective
—that is, strangely like our imple-
ments,—or discovers on forgotten cave-
walls drawings which indicate a remark-
able eye for things as they still are.
Yet the mass impression remains, that

this life was once a matter of chance or luck, and experience was unforeseeable; that the race-mind cleared very slowly; and that we are the first to imagine a universe of complete and unalterable law.

Our complacent attitude toward primitive man has of late been fostered by certain gifted classical scholars, chief among them Professor Gilbert Murray and Miss Jane Harrison, who with the help of anthropology have recreated that dim world which lay behind Greek letters. The beautiful logic by which these scholars reach their results increases our conceit that reason is a modern instrument, while the world they picture, a hopeless tangle of religion and superstition, of necromancy and the arts, reassures us as to what we have risen from. Against that sombre background Homer, once thought primitive, seems

recent and enlightened. Professor J. A.
K. Thompson, in his *Studies in the Odyssey*, published in 1914, provides us with
numerous examples. The Homeric epics
are full of what are called "expurgations"
of earlier legend. Those stories of bodily
transformation which Ovid gathered up
as fairy tales in his *Metamorphoses*, the
primitive Greek took quite literally; but
since the Homeric way of seeing life
would not countenance this make-believe, the transformations were "ex-
purgated" by being turned into similes.
When we read in the *Odyssey*, "So spake
she and departed, the grey-eyed Athena,
and like an eagle of the sea she flew
away," we surmise that in an older story
the goddess turned herself into the sea-
eagle. The Homeric conscience is re-
luctant to transmit this account of the
outer world; the most that can be conceded is a resemblance between Athena

and the sea-eagle. Sometimes, it must
be confessed, the concession is more
startling than the original transformation. When Hera and Athena came to
the plains of Troy to aid the Greeks, we
are told that "the goddesses went their
way" into battle "with step like unto
turtle-doves." The explanation is that
as attendants on Zeus, the goddesses had
originally been imagined in the form of
his sacred doves. The most helpful
example, however, of the Homeric expurgation is the story of Dolon, in the
tenth book of the *Iliad*. When Dolon
set out to spy on the Greeks, he "cast
on his shoulders his crooked bow, and
put on thereover the skin of a grey wolf,
and on his head a helm of ferret-skin,
and took a sharp javelin, and went on his
way to the ships." In the *Iliad* that
grey wolf-skin is only a garment. But
in the *Rhesus* of Euripides, which appears

to follow the earlier legends, Dolon explains his device to the chorus:

"Over my back a wolf-skin will I draw,
    And the brute's gaping jaws shall frame my
        head:
    Its forefeet will I fasten to my hands,
    Its legs to mine; the wolf's four-footed gait
    I'll mimic, baffling so our enemies,
    While near the trench and pale of ships I am;
    But whenso to a lone spot come my feet,
    Two-footed will I walk."

Here the wolf-skin is a disguise, which, though not in itself magical, carries us nearer to that primitive age when stealthy men, for their own purposes, changed into were-wolves, and when every wild beast, therefore, implied a fearful possibility that it was a man transformed.

From such illuminating glimpses into the early world we make the conclusion that primitive man dwelt in mystery, that he was fond of make-believe, that he had a highly developed sense of magic—in other words, that he looked for delightful shortcuts and escapes from the facts of life, whereas we look for the law which explains and controls the facts. But the truth probably is that primitive man had no sense of magic whatever; when he busied himself with his incantations and his hocus-pocus, he probably had a quite modern sense of cause and effect. To us he seems a magician, because his method of getting at the cause or at the effect was not ours; but he had no measure by which to judge himself. He consulted the medicine-man as we consult the doctor, and his faith was no more shaken than ours is by a failure to cure. It is the conception of magic, not the conception of cause and effect, which has grown with time and enlightenment. Now, and only now, can we realize how much of primitive science was really magic; but in the

essential desire to have a science—that
is, to control and ameliorate our destiny
by calculated means, it is not clear that
we differ from our ultimate ancestors.

In one respect, however, we ought to
differ from them. If time has provided
us with a criticism of magic, of illegitimate
and ineffective attempts at power, it
should have taught us also to admire
what is lawful, effective, and true. If
primitive literature, recording an incomprehensible world, yearned after magic, our records, of a world understood,
should be full of wonder—that is, full
of idealizing joy in the truth and in the
beauty before our eyes. Time should
have distinguished us so from earlier
man, because the ability to wonder comes
late. To be sure, the Rousseau senti-
mentalists imagined the savage as contemplating the heavens and the earth
beneath with astonishment and awe, and

they drew substance for their fancy from
the supposed exaltation of spirit with
which young children make their acquaintance with this planet. But nothing in our observation of children or in
the anthropologist's observation of primitive men, would allow much truth in
this old doctrine; the very contrary
seems to be the fact—that only the
sophisticated can appreciate the miracles
that are actually before our eyes. Children take their world for granted; when
we disclose some amazement at life, some
awe of facts, it is a sign that we are no
longer children. Moreover, we wonder
only at what lies on the border of our
experience; what is totally beyond us
we still take for granted. The unclothed
savage of Borneo is brought to the settle-
ments and treated to a ride in a motor-
car. Knowing nothing of such things,
he is neither surprised nor interested,

but lets the car, like gravitation, do its work. But he gapes for hours at a steel hammer or a serviceable saw.

Our pity, then, for primitive man's defective science, hardly covers the situation. Surely we can forgive the first comers for taking hold by the wrong handles; we still revise our methods. But what if we, who think of the universe as a realm of law, feel toward it no great wonder, not even a hearty approval, but still yearn after a magic, after an escape of some kind from the inexorable logic of life; what if we, who know the majestic fidelity wherewith nature keeps her elements true to themselves, still desire, in the most spiritual things, an outworn alchemy! I wish to raise the question whether the literature even of modern times, far from expressing wonder, does not express a certain unwillingness to face the world we know; whether it does not display a tendency to make use—a more subtle use—of those primitive transformations which Homer rejected; whether it does not show a perverse delight in substituting the miraculous for the normal—preferring, that is, to give such an account of the outer and inner world as we know to be false, instead of the account which we know to be true.

I ask your attention, then, to the inconsistency between our faith that the universe is orderly and wonderful, and our pleasure in that literature which represents life as miraculous and magical —between, that is, our conviction that miracles are the measure of wonder, and our disposition to treat them as the products of magic. The difference is great. If we love the poetry of life, there is a sense in which we cannot get along without miracles; without them as

a language to talk with, we cannot express that profound wonder at common
facts which is the sign of enlightened
manhood. For this reason we are un-
willing to give up fairy stories or the
legend of Santa Claus, until some other
language is provided for dreams and aspirations. We boldly make use of miracles to express or interpret life. But
to account for life by miracles is stupid
and unnecessary. Plutarch says that
on the farm of Pericles a ram was found
having a single horn. Lampon the
soothsayer declared that Pericles, by this
omen, would become sole ruler in Athens.
But an annoying person named Anaxagoras split the ram's skull in two, and
showed that by a peculiar formation the
horn had to grow single. So Anaxagoras
confuted the soothsayer. But later Pericles did become ruler, and the soothsayer recovered his authority. Plutarch's

comment is that they were both right, for one explained how the horn grew, and the other explained what it meant— just as, when the dinner-bell rings, we know how the sound is produced, and we know what it means. It would be stupid, however—though I believe some philosophers have been guilty—to confuse the interpretation with the cause, to say it is the significance of the dinner-bell that is ringing it. The quarrel with the miraculous in literature, therefore, is only with the miraculous when used as magic—as a wilful substitute for that continuity of cause and effect which outside of literature we believe in.

II

Of this kind of magic it is easy to find illustrations in medieval literature. Certain well-known French lays of the twelfth or thirteenth century picture just such an irresponsible, accidental world as we usually ascribe to primitive man. In one story a fair lady is shut up in a tower, that she may not see her lover. As she is bemoaning her fate, a magnificent eagle flies through the narrow window, and lighting on the chamber floor, turns into a handsome young man, her persevering suitor. In another story a fair lady is imprisoned, and her true knight, instead of coming himself in a magic disguise, sends to her a wonderful swan, which flies back and forth between the two, carrying always a letter beneath his plumage. In another story a man confides to his wife that during his frequent absences from home he turns himself into a were-wolf, and she straightway contrives that the next time he shall not resume his human form. Here are such transformations as we glanced at in pre-Homeric legend, but no attempt at the Homeric expurgation is here, unless the swan in the second story be such. Far from desiring any expurgation, the medieval audience may have been glad enough that literature should not give an accurate account of their life. They may have liked mystery for its own sake, as there is little reason to think primitive man ever did. Their faculty of wonder, we know, they exercised in contemplating the world to come; if, as we suspect, they rejoiced in this present life also with an almost renaissance paganism, at least they rejoiced surreptitiously. It is incredible that they did not recognize as magic such episodes as we have just summarized; and if this material was as frankly magical to them as it now seems to us, it is a fact of some importance that the middle ages left us few pictures of the world as it was

actually seen. We are sometimes told
that in those unlucky centuries the
Church imposed miracles and legends on
secular ignorance. Whether or not those
centuries were unlucky, a reading of these
secular stories suggests wonder that more
miracles and legends were not imposed
on the Church.

But however the twelfth century may
have understood its literature, there is
little doubt that the fourteenth century
liked a certain class of stories which
must have been recognized as false to
experience. I refer to those tales of
reckless or scandalous love—merry tales,
as the Elizabethan translators would call
them—such as Boccaccio included in a
part of his famous collection. Their real
immorality is not often observed, nor is
it obvious in any single story; but when
one reflects on all such stories as a class,
whether in the *Decameron* or in other

collections, the amazing thing is that though they picture villainy, cruelty, and treachery, they picture no effects of villainy, cruelty, or treachery; their escapades continue to be merry; there is no hint of possible tragedy for man nor of pity for woman. To be sure, the medieval story-teller does chronicle sorrow, and he does treat womanhood sympathetically, but never when dealing with such themes as we are thinking of. Patient Griselda is a medieval heroine; Tess of the D'Urbervilles is not. The middle ages, moreover, defined tragedy as a fall from good fortune to bad, and comedy as a rise from bad fortune to good; doubtless God punished the wicked and rewarded the righteous, but in His own miraculous way, not in the inherent consequences of a moral choice. It is only by the caprice of her husband that Griselda is rewarded; to a dramatic

imagination she seems not so much rewarded as tortured.

In the Renaissance there was a conception of virtue which carried with it
a belief, if not in a miraculous world in
general, at least in a special magic or
talisman for the individual. To the
Greek mind a virtue was a state, a condition between two extremes, and Renaissance philosophers, piously accepting
Aristotle's terms, continued to speak of
virtue as a mean. But the imaginative
literature of the Renaissance, in which
we get the less academic account of life,
has a tendency to speak of virtue, not as
a quality or condition, but as a thing, to
be acquired and possessed. The Renaissance man is not courageous—he has
courage; the Renaissance woman is not
beautiful—she has beauty. Whether this
idea of virtue brought about the belief in
a magic or talisman, or whether the

belief in a magic, helped by Platonic ideas, brought about this conception of virtue, it is at least clear that beauty, courage, friendship, or any other virtue, is often treated in Renaissance literature as a magical instrument, like the enchanted spears and shields of medieval romance. In the Provençal tradition beauty was such a magic. The story of Aucassin and Nicolete, which though medieval in date is renaissance in spirit, tells how Nicolete passed by the door where a pilgrim lay sick, and the sight of her made him a well man. In the *Faerie Queene*, when Artegal is jousting with Britomart, he happens to strike off the front of her helmet. Her divine beauty causes his sword to fall powerless, and he is taken captive. In *Paradise Lost*, when the serpent approaches to tempt Eve, her loveliness renders the devil, for one moment, stupidly good.

Nicolete and Britomart had a permanent magic; Eve's beauty was effective only for a moment. Milton was skeptical of magic, not only because he came late in the Renaissance, but because he had an unusual intellect, and a mathematician's sense for order. In him the tradition of virtue as a talisman or miraculous instrument temporarily died out. For example, chivalry had fostered a belief in the magic of being right, the magic on which the institution of judicial combat was founded. He who had the right in any encounter must of necessity prevail. This institution was accepted throughout Spenser's *Faerie Queene;* unless they had first committed a sin or fallen into an error, the good champions could not be overcome by the powers of evil. We remember, in passing, how Scott accommodated this large faith to modern skepticism, killing off the Templar by a stroke of apoplexy just in time to save Ivanhoe. It might have been thought that Shakspere, who was closer than most men to the realities of experience, would have taken the edge off the miracle, as Scott did; but in *As You Like It* Orlando, having a just cause, is able to throw the professional wrestler. It remained for Milton to reject magic. To see how far he advanced beyond Spenser, for example, we have but to imagine how Spenser would have written *Comus.* The heroine of the poem, another Britomart, possessing the heavenly virtue of chastity, would have been armed against the spells of the sorcerer. All that Milton claims in the end, though he starts out bravely, is that the lady's soul was unharmed, though Comus did enchant her body. This concession is larger than at first might appear, for it contradicts the fine boast of the elder brother, who in the poem speaks for Milton—

"Against the threats
Of malice or of sorcery, or that power
Which erring men call chance, this I hold firm:
Virtue may be assailed, but never hurt,
Surprised by unjust force, but not enthralled.

Yet virtue is enthralled, and it is the grace of heaven, not the lady's innocence, that releases her. In *Paradise Lost* Milton still clings, poet-like, to the magic of beauty, but the magic of being right he gives over, preferring to read man's fortunes dramatically, as the inevitable result of his choice among fixed laws. He holds to the dramatic attitude in *Sampson Agonistes*, although he does represent the giant's strength as still residing in his hair. This survival of primitive magic, however, is only figurative, a symbol of moral power lost and regained. Having given his allegiance to what he believed was a righteous cause, and having seen that cause collapse, Milton could but agree with Sir Thomas Browne, that a man may be in as just possession of truth as of a city, and yet be forced to surrender.

III

But the career of magic was not over. Milton rejected it, as Homer had done, as Scott did later, and many another individual here and there; but it is not for their rejection of magic that Homer or Milton or Scott has been widely praised. We have advanced far enough to ask that our talismans be of a less obvious kind than satisfied men a thousand years ago, but a talisman of some kind we still delight in. Witness three novelists, undeniably great, who are supposed to account for life genuinely and honestly, yet who show a certain reluctance to accept the universe of order, and hark back rather to the old magical transformation.

One of these novelists is Fielding. Criticism has stressed his manliness, his insistence on frankness, his ability to deal with a fact. Yet in none of his stories, except *Jonathan Wild,* does he treat his heroes as though character were really conditioned by causes and consequences. We watch the good and the bad traits in Tom Jones, for the first twenty-five years of his life, and then we are asked to believe that, once happily married, he reformed, and his faults not only disappeared, but obligingly left no traces. In *Amelia* we must believe the same miracle of Booth, with the added difficulty that he is older when he reforms. In the minor details of both stories, as also in *Joseph Andrews,* there is a lucky juxtaposition of events to help out the character, which suggests the fairy godmother rather than the observer of this world. No ill effects result from bad choices, and good fortune is not the result of wisdom in the characters, but of benevolence in the author. Fielding has had his reputation from his hearty interest in life and his advance in verisimilitude over his predecessors. Looking back now, however, we see that his interest in life was neither wide nor deep, and that he had no use for the conception of the world as a sequence of inexorable justice; he preferred to think of it as a career where manliness was a sufficient talisman—where the effects of conduct suspended themselves for a possibly erring heart, so long as it was stout.

To make a similar criticism of Dickens requires some resolution, for he enlists our loyalty as Fielding never does

MAGIC AND WONDER

Our affection convinces us rightly that whatever the literary critic may pronounce upon *David Copperfield* or *Old Curiosity Shop* or *Our Mutual Friend*, the emotions which those books stirred in us were noble. The fact is that Dickens uses the miraculous in both ways at once, as an interpretation and as an account of life. With him the same incident serves to state an ideal and to chronicle a fact. If only his facts had been correct, he would have illustrated the perfect formula of art. As it is, we fall in love with his ideals; and we learn better than to believe his picture of life. He accounted for experience, and explained it, by the simple magic of goodness. Before a good man, the problems of this world melt away. There is a wide difference between this goodness and the old chivalric magic of being right. If one is right, at least one is in unconscious

accord with the facts and the laws of
the universe. In Dickens the admirable
characters are often mistaken, even hor-
ribly in the wrong, but they are good,
and so long as they remain good they
excite admiration and surmount difficulties. The illustrations of this magic
occur in the most characteristic parts of
Dickens' work—in the *Christmas Carol*,
for example. To read this story for its
emotions is to learn generosity and
brotherly love; but how disconcerting
to learn our virtues from a false picture
of life! Do misers like Scrooge repent?
Can anyone turn over a new leaf and
undo all his past? And does such goodness as Tiny Tim's or Bob Cratchit's
really solve the difficulties of their situation as completely as Dickens represents?
The pity that we feel for Tiny Tim is a
tribute to what is true in the story;
the comfortable optimism with which

we put down the book, is evidence of some trick of magic, some eluding of truth—for looking at men and women around us, we are convinced that such satisfaction is not reached that way. Besides, we have learned to think that people in poverty or misery are still in trouble even though they are brave about it; if we could agree that goodness is a talisman, we might as well give up all social work, on the ground that the worthy poor are as happy as possible, and the unhappy poor must be unworthy.

What Dickens has done, then, is to state his ideals in terms of what pretends to be real experience. Our admiration cannot be withheld from the ideals, nor can our intelligence endorse the account of life. If it is a fairy story that we are reading, we ought not to be deceived into mistaking it for history. There is reason to think, however, that Dickens did not consider it a disadvantage to be the victim of illusion. At least he portrayed many "illusionists," as a German scholar called them, who tabulated and classified them all. Mr. Pickwick, Mrs. Nickleby, Swiveller, Tom Pinch, David Copperfield, and of course Mr. Micawber, are among the illusionists. The French critic Taine made the same point by saying that many characters in Dickens have a touch of insanity.

In the world as Dickens represents it, these illusioned characters get on very well, but in the real world they come to grief. Of such disillusion Thackeray is the kindliest example. At least he represents a partial reaction from the magic of goodness; he can no longer believe in it, but he wishes with all his heart he could. What really happens to absolute goodness in this world is portrayed, not in Bob Cratchit, nor in David Copperfield, but in Colonel Newcome. With magic Thackeray is convinced, we might say, that the novel should have nothing to do, yet he devotes his art to no religion of wonder. Because he has so gently and persuasively corrected Dickens' picture of life, at the same time endorsing, as it were, his ideals, Thackeray has had much reputation for wisdom and modernness. Yet in the cardinal emotions of wonder and delight he is not modern at all; the logic of character, the unalterable order, whereby Colonel Newcome suffered for his mistakes, however excellent his motives—this saddens Thackeray, even though he is in honor bound to present it. For an ordered universe he has no love, nor any passion for the career of the mind. Perhaps it is only his sentimentality that hides from us the materialism in his picture of life—the implication that the good are victims of inevitable laws; whereas they are really victims of their own ignorance. The laws of human nature, if Colonel Newcome were only wise enough to make them the instruments of happiness, would seem reliable, to wonder at, rather than inexorable, to fear.

Of stories and plays written in our own time it is enough to say that few of them show any persuasion that there is consequence in the world. If you open any of the numerous manuals which tell you how to write fiction, you may read that actions should be motivated, that there should be reasons why things happen—as though cause and effect were subdivisions of the literary art. Few of our contemporary writers seem to practise this instruction, and still fewer of their readers know whether they practise it or not. We have with us still, of course, special schools of

fiction, which insist on a precise or a
continuous or an unselected rendering of
experience — realistic and naturalistic
schools; and individual masters of real-
ism or naturalism from time to time
captivate many readers. But even these
individual successes, added together, seem
to make no total impression on the reading world. In contemporary fiction characters slough off the past, serpent-like,
and emerge brighter than ever; or they
change their nature in a twinkling; and
it seems that few readers seriously protest against the miracle. Our supposed
faith in the logic of personality, our
faith that a given character will act in a
certain way, our faith especially that a
man's conduct or occupation influences
his character, that he is marked by what
he does—all this we seem to have sur-
rendered, substituting in its place a
misty benevolence, a magic of the Dick-

ens type, a persuasion that any character, viewed sympathetically, will seem, or will actually become, as admirable as any other character.

One illustration may be found in the stories of the underworld, where the professional criminal or wrongdoer is shown in the final paradox to be essentially righteous and permanently reformed. We are convinced, of course, that to be a professional crook will in the end lead to some moral deterioration. We read with pleasure, however, these fables which keep the soul of the crook unspotted from his own conduct. Our pleasure is based on a fine humaneness, on the undoubted fact that criminals are largely manufactured or at least encouraged by circumstances, and that few of them were originally bad at heart. But this doctrine, excellent as a vantage-point from which to enter upon social responsibility and rescue, has been stretched in our fiction until it misrepresents the consequences of wrongdoing, and even diminishes, strangely enough, that sense of social responsibility from which it sprang. We felt to blame for letting our fellow-man become a criminal, but after the story or the play has demonstrated how excellent morally the criminal is, we feel less guilty. In such tales, however, there is always an inconsistency; the hero is singled out for admiration, but his comrades in guilt are saved by no miracle—so much is conceded to our general knowledge of the facts.

Another illustration may be drawn from a very different region of interest, from those stories or plays, like *The Passing of the Third Floor Back*, or *The Servant in the House*, which show the miraculous influence of a perfect character. In such fiction a stranger is represented as entering a community, a group of people formed and settled, and by the magic of his presence transmuting them into quite different persons. This kind of story must express some precious ideal, or it would not be so tenderly popular; but as a picture of life it is both incorrect and immoral, for it both contradicts our experience and relieves us—provided we can entertain the stranger—of responsibility for our conduct. To be sure, the public thinks this type of story far from immoral—rather a religious parable, for does not the author suggest that the stranger is Christ? And does not that suggestion explain the miracles? But here we see how an inclination to magic befuddles our ordinary intelligence. Because the stranger converts everybody he meets, we think he is Christ-like, forgetting that the

New Testament gives no such account
of Christ.

IV

Perhaps the contrast has been in-
dicated sufficiently between the universe
of law which we are supposed to believe
in, and the world of magic which we
like to read about. What does this inconsistency mean? Perhaps it is rash
to venture on so large a question in so
short a space, but in this balancing of
magic against wonder a conviction steals
on one that the love of magic, though it
may be stupid, indicates something far
higher than stupidity. The connota-
tions of the words themselves convince
us. Magic suggests power, however ob-
tained, whereas wonder suggests no power at all. Is there such merit in enlightenment if one is to be, after all,

only an enlightened bystander? The magician at least wanted control of experience — and so do we! Magic sought to engage the help of alien forces, foreign gods, in the problems of this world; we, believing that no gods are alien to our universe, ought logically to make the remotest force effective in our daily aspirations; we cannot stop with a passive wonder. Or if we do, our sympathies, and the sympathy of our fellows, will return to magic, which with all its defects dreamt of power.

When we consider how many noble intellects have tried in vain to take from the race its love of magic, and to teach it instead the habit of wonder, the long failure can be explained, I think, by the fact that the ideal of wonder has rarely included the ideal of control, without which we refuse to be fascinated. This is true of the philosophers, who though

they have sought to correct all haphazard and irresponsible impressions of
the universe, yet have so far failed, in
that they have not greatly disturbed
man's love of magical stories. Some of
them, Francis Bacon, for example, have
opened up visions of scientific control
more magical than magic itself; we shall
owe it to them eventually that our magic
and our wonder have become identical.
But most philosophers have been content
to attack the ignorance of magic without
satisfying its aspiration; and the wonder
which they would substitute, though
nobly imaginative, has stopped short of
that power men yearn for. Lucretius
serves for example, whose poem on the
Nature of Things sought to take away
our fear of death by removing our faith
in immortality—or, as he would say, our
superstition. This intended service has
not roused the gratitude of mankind.

What stirs us in the poem is the vision of an ordered world, and an impassioned rebuke that the vision has not stirred us before. To feed our sense of wonder we have had recourse to fairy tales; but, says the poet, "Look up at the bright and unsullied hue of heaven, and the stars which it holds within it, wandering about, and the moon and the sun's light of dazzling brilliancy; if all these things were now for the first time suddenly presented to mortals, what could have been named that would be more marvelous?" Here is an escape from ignorance, if you please, a sense of wonder in the presence of the actual universe; but when we have felt this wonder, what next? Having got rid of our superstitions, shall we then be ready to die?

The same criticism can be made of Milton, the one English poet comparable

with Lucretius in loftiness and fervor.
His sense of reality, as we saw, kept him
from believing in magic; his special gift,
it seems, was for wonder on an infinite
scale. But he stops with wonder; he
would not have mankind seek knowledge
for the magic purpose of control. When
Adam voices his suspicion that the sun,
the moon, and the stars, are not circling
the earth, as they appear to be doing,
for the sole uneconomic purpose of fur-
nishing light for one man and his wife,
Raphael replies with a superb summary
of both the Ptolemaic and the Coper-
nican theories, but he advises Adam not
to bother his head with either hypothesis,
nor to prosecute any scientific inquiry.
The great Architect, he says,

"Did wisely to conceal, and not divulge
  His secrets to be scann'd by them who ought
  Rather admire. . . .
  Solicit not thy thoughts with matters hid,
  Leave them to God above, Him serve and fear."

IN LITERATURE

That Milton, himself pre-eminently a thinker and a student, should have represented the powers of good as opposed to enquiry, has greatly puzzled his admirers. We should like to find an argument on the other side in Adam's reply to the angel,

> "To know
> That which before us lies in daily life
> Is the prime wisdom."

We should like to translate this speech into a praise of practical science, of enquiry which has for object the control of one's destiny. But there is nothing in the context to aid this interpretation.

If the philosophers have not lured us to a reasonable view of life, the satirists have not driven us to it. Wherever satire has dealt with man's ignorance, it has attacked magic in some form. Even magic-lovers themselves, as to some extent Fielding and Thackeray were, have appealed to the inexorable order when they wrote satirically, as in *Jonathan Wild* and *Barry Lyndon*. The stock in trade of George Bernard Shaw today is our persisting trust in magic formulas. The substance of his art is but to prick that bubble. In *Androcles and the Lion*, for example, he gives a reading of Christian martyrdom in what professes to be the unchanging law of character; his audience wonder why he should have demonstrated the obvious, and they remark as they go home that he is losing his old sparkle. But they have applauded with spontaneous and unembarrassed delight that moment in the play where the lion refuses to eat Androcles—which proves, I suppose, that they have fallen into Shaw's trap. Yet with all this clever exposing of our inconsistencies, the satirist gives us no vision of what

life would be like, were we to make intelligent use of the laws we profess to
believe in.

Here and there, however, poets have
given us glimpses of the vision. Such
a poet is Shelley. We do not usually
praise him for a sense of fact. Yet few
men have tried so honestly to give their
enthusiasms to the proper objects, or
have contemplated with such genuine
rapture the control over experience which
a knowledge of nature's order should
give. His education in science was amateurish and fragmentary, but no special-
ist conceives more clearly or more rap-
turously the magic possibilities of exact
knowledge. For Shelley, science was to
be the key to nature's secrets, and those
secrets, once known, were to subject
nature to man. The fullest expression
of this faith is in *Prometheus Unbound*,
the last act of which, in praise of what

may be called scientific living, might be
read as a commentary on *The Newcomes*.

"Man, one harmonious soul of many a soul,
   Whose nature is its own divine control,
   Where all things flow to all, as rivers to the sea;
Familiar acts are beautiful through love;
Labor, and pain, and grief, in life's green grove
Sport like tame beasts, none knew how gentle
      they could be!
  . . . . . .

All things confess man's strength—Through the
      cold mass
Of marble and of color his dreams pass;
Bright threads whence mothers weave the robes
      their children wear;
Language is a perpetual Orphic song,
Which rules with Dædal harmony a throng
Of thoughts and forms, which else senseless and
      shapeless were.

The lightning is his slave; heaven's utmost deep
Gives up her stars, and like a flock of sheep
They pass before his eye, are numbered, and
      roll on!
The tempest is his steed, he strides the air;
And the abyss shouts from her depth laid bare,
Heaven, hast thou secrets? Man unveils me;
      I have none.

Such a poet, to name a second, is
Emerson. He, also, is not famous for
any grasp on reality. His fame, however,
does him injustice. He was indeed a
mystic, and much of his teaching seems
to belittle the facts of life, the terms on
which we move in this present world.
But he did not belittle facts, nor under-
value whatever is actual. There is no
real power, he taught, which is not
based on nature, and the beginning of
power is the belief that things go not
by luck, but by law. Even when the
mystic in him was uppermost, he often
meant in a nobly practical way what
we have taken as an extravagance of
idealism. "Hitch your wagon to a star."
We translate "aim high"—but that was
not his meaning. He meant that we
should be scientific, if you choose—that
having learned to wonder at the laws
and forces of the universe, we should

then turn the laws to our advantage and should ourselves control the forces. These are his words: "I admire the skill which, on the seashore, makes the tides drive the wheels and grind corn, and which thus engages the assistance of the moon, like a hired hand, to grind, and wind, and pump, and saw, and split stone, and roll iron. Now that is the wisdom of a man, in every instance of his labor, to hitch his wagon to a star."

Here is an invitation to a greater power than magic, and here, I think, is a fore-taste of what poetry may be. Lucretius stood in awe before the universe, but he stood aloof; Shelley and Emerson, modern of the moderns, beheld man entering into control of a vaster universe than the Roman poet merely contemplated. When literature expresses the miracle of that control, our common life will be

transfigured in wonder, our dreams will
lie, not in the impossible, but in the
path of our happy destiny, and the gods
will walk with us.

THE END